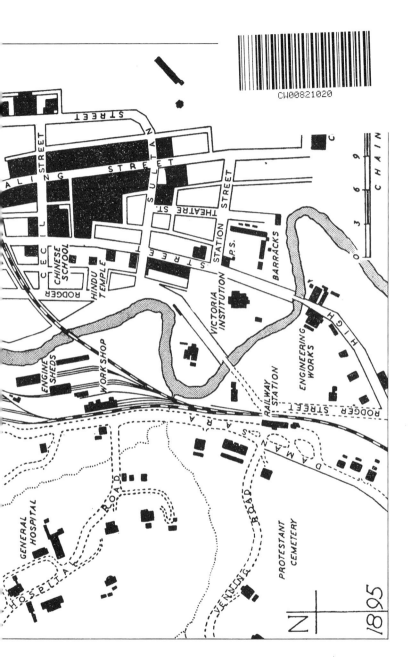

IMAGES OF ASIA

Old Kuala Lumpur

Titles in the series

Old Kuala Lumpur

J. M. GULLICK

KUALA LUMPUR
OXFORD UNIVERSITY PRESS
OXFORD SINGAPORE NEW YORK
1994

Oxford University Press

Oxford New York
Athens Auckland Bangkok Bombay
Calcutta Cape Town Dar es Salaam Delhi
Florence Hong Kong Istanbul Karachi
Kuala Lumpur Madras Madrid Melbourne
Mexico City Nairobi Paris Singapore
Taipei Tokyo Toronto

and associated companies in

Berlin Ibadan

Oxford is a trade mark of Oxford University Press

Published in the United States
by Oxford University Press, New York

© Oxford University Press 1994
First published 1994

British Library Cataloguing in Publication Data
Data available

Library of Congress Cataloging-in-Publication Data

Gullick, J. M.
Old Kuala Lumpur/J. M. Gullick.
p.   cm.—(Images of Asia)
Includes bibliographical references and index.
ISBN 967 65 3073 5:
1. Kuala Lumpur (Malaysia)—History. I. Title. II. Series.
DS599. K8G8495   1994
959.5'1—dc20
94–26324
CIP

Typeset by Indah Photosetting Centre Sdn. Bhd., Malaysia
Printed by Kyodo Printing Co. (S) Pte. Ltd., Singapore
Published by Oxford University Press,
19–25, Jalan Kuchai Lama, 58200 Kuala Lumpur, Malaysia

Preface

KUALA LUMPUR only emerges into the full daylight of recorded history in 1880, when it became the State capital of Selangor. Until the early 1870s officials and businessmen in the towns of the Straits Settlements referred vaguely to 'Klang', meaning the entire Klang Valley, as an important centre of tin mining. The name 'Kuala Lumpur' was by then in local use but did not appear generally in contemporary records until after the civil war (1867–73) was over. Thus, it was as recently as 1934 that the eminent scholar, Sir Richard Winstedt, writing a history of Selangor before colonial rule, only referred in passing to Kuala Lumpur as the scene of fighting during the civil war, and did not once mention Yap Ah Loy, of whose existence he was apparently unaware.

In 1936, however, S. M. Middlebrook, a Chinese-speaking administrator, chanced on an account of Yap Ah Loy in an old Chinese periodical. He found it so interesting that he set about gathering scraps of information from what other sources he could find with a view to writing a short biography of Yap Ah Loy for the *Journal of the Malayan Branch of the Royal Asiatic Society* (*JMBRAS*). When Middlebrook, with many other Europeans, was interned in Changi Gaol in Singapore in 1942, he took his unfinished work with him. Unfortunately, his Chinese language documents aroused the suspicions of the Japanese, who believed—quite wrongly—that internees were passing information through Singapore Chinese to assist allied commando raids. Middlebrook was one of the internees who were rounded up in the savage 'Double Tenth' affair in 1943, and he died of the ill-treatment which he suffered. His papers were confiscated and some were lost, but the actual manuscript of his biography was returned to his cell and preserved until 1945 by his friends. It was, however, much altered in Middlebrook's difficult handwriting and no one but his widow could have, as she did, decipher it to produce a legible typescript. His story of Yap Ah Loy ended in 1873, since the Chinese sources he used recorded that the gallant hero had emerged on the winning side in the war; they believed he had then lived happily on until his death in 1885.

The editor of *JMBRAS* asked the author of this book, who knew nothing whatever of the subject, whether a concluding chapter on the period 1873–85 could be compiled to complete the biography. In response to a casual enquiry made to the State Secretary, Selangor, the latter said that he did not know whether the extant Selangor Government files went back as far as 1885 but he would make enquiries. It took three office messengers a long, hot afternoon to bring down from an attic (in the Bangunan Sultan Abdul Samad), where they had long since been forgotten, some 10,000–20,000 files of the period 1875–85 (a file of that period contained a single letter and the reply; a new file was opened if the matter was continued).

These archives yielded much information on Yap Ah Loy and Kuala Lumpur, since the town was the powerhouse of the Selangor economy, even in hard times, and Yap Ah Loy, until 1880, had virtually sole charge; administrators from Klang merely came to visit him now and again. By the time the research was done, the Selangor Government had plans to use the vacant storage room for other purposes and proposed to destroy the 'old files'. However, Professor Northcote Parkinson (later world famous for 'Parkinson's Law') was then head of the History Department of the University of Malaya in Singapore. On learning what was intended, he intervened (his indignation reverberated from Singapore to Kuala Lumpur like the Krakatoa volcanic eruption of 1883). The records are now carefully preserved (and have been indexed) at the Arkib Negara.

That was not the end of the discovery of sources of information on pre-1880 Kuala Lumpur. In 1942 Frank Swettenham had published his memoirs, with a brief passage on his first visit to Kuala Lumpur in 1872. He had returned to work in Selangor in 1874 and his Selangor journal, in which he described his second visit to Kuala Lumpur in March 1875, was found a century later in the small reference library at Malaysia House (the former Malay

States Information Agency) in Trafalgar Square. Swettenham's Perak and Selangor journals, edited by Dr P. L. Burns, were published by the Oxford University Press in 1975.

At about that time, E. Douglas Potter, then a civil servant in Edinburgh, wrote to the British Association of Malaya (BAM) in London to say that a friend who had lived in Malaya had, while visiting his house, seen the four volumes of his grandfather's manuscript diary written when the latter was an administrator in Malaya around 1880. Was the diary, preserved merely as a family possession, of any historical interest? The Secretary of the BAM was inclined to be dismissive but, fortunately, sought advice. Thus, we discovered the working journal of Captain Bloomfield Douglas, Resident of Selangor from 1876 to 1882. Douglas made periodic visits to Kuala Lumpur and was in constant contact with Yap Ah Loy. In 1880 he, in fact, moved to Kuala Lumpur, where he lived until his retirement in 1882. A facsimile (xerox) copy of the complete diary has, by permission of Potter, been deposited at the Rhodes House Library at Oxford.

Since some emphasis has been placed on the personal role of Yap Ah Loy, as head of the Chinese community of Kuala Lumpur, the picture of its history in his time should be put in perspective (as the opening chapter seeks to do) by reminding the reader that Malay settlers and miners had developed the interior of Selangor in the first half of the nineteenth century, and they continued to play a leading part both in the power struggles and the economic vicissitudes which followed. Chinese mining was built upon and ran in parallel with Malay agriculture—and also tin mining and trade. Early Kuala Lumpur was made by the combined efforts of two communities.

In accordance with the publishers' format for the 'Images of Asia' series, this book is—to its great benefit—well illustrated by more than forty plates, both in colour and black and white. These have been garnered from several sources, and it is a pleasure to acknowledge the help received in what at the outset seemed a hopeless search. Kuala Lumpur is not as richly endowed as, say, Penang with contemporary artistic records of its early years. However, this book has the incidental merit of reproducing (from the beginning of this century onwards) the work of Mary Barnard, Dorothea Aldworth, R. D. Jackson, Kathleen (Russell) Gemmill, Mohamed Hoessin Enas, and Victor Chin. The illustrations also include photographs, notably from the work of the staff of the Singapore firm of G. R. Lambert & Co., pioneers in Malayan photography. Much of the early photography now survives in the form of postcards.

The captions identify the source of each plate, but the publishers and the author would like to express their personal thanks to Victor Chin, John Falconer, Airlie Gascoyne, John Nicholson, Tristan Russell, Revd Charles Samuel, Michael Sweet, Steven Tan, and Shell Companies in Malaysia.

If this brief narrative of eighty years inclines the reader to look further afield, the Select Bibliography lists the published works from which this book has been compiled.

Essex   J. M. GULLICK
May 1994

Contents

1
How It Began

KUALA LUMPUR began as a very small settlement on the river bank through which the surrounding tin mines received labourers and the food to support them. By the same route they sent back the ingots of tin which they had produced. Above the junction of the Klang River with the Gombak—more a stream than a river—heavy river boats could not go (Plate 1). Hence, the boats making the four-day transit to and from the town of Klang offloaded or onloaded their cargoes at this point. It was close to the mines and goods could be carried over jungle tracks on the backs of porters.

Malays, mainly Sumatran immigrants, had long before settled on the banks of the Klang River to grow food, to collect jungle produce such as rattan (a useful substitute for rope), and to work alluvial surface tin ore deposits. As far back as the 1820s we hear

1. The *kuala* (river junction) which gives the town its name.
    (Steven Tan)

1

of Malay villages such as Petaling. This washing for tin in the beds of streams, to earn a little money between harvesting the paddy crop and planting the next, only showed how much more could be gained by more intensive methods. In 1857 Raja Abdullah, the business-like Malay chief who governed—more or less—the entire Klang Valley from the estuary to the watershed which divides Selangor from Pahang, sent a party of eighty-seven Chinese miners, recruited with the backing of merchants in the Straits Settlements, to mine for tin in the upper valley, then known vaguely as Ulu Klang. The party disembarked at the Klang–Gombak junction, and set off to prospect. As strangers in a foreign land, disposed to believe that success or failure depended on the favour or emnity of local genii, they recruited Malay magicians (*pawang*) who might be counted on to have a good working relationship with the spirits of the place. A *pawang* had a smattering of practical geology, gained by experience, to supplement his incantations. If he found tin, he then gave additional service for his consultant's fee by imparting to the superstitious Chinese miners various rules of conduct by which they might avoid giving offence to the local deities. On a Chinese mine it was forbidden to wear shoes or to carry an umbrella (it was cynically suggested that these taboos kept Chinese financial backers from making on-site inspections). There were others, however, which defy rational explanation, such as, a man must not work in the mine with only his bathing cloth around his body; he must wear trousers. If he took off his hat and put it on the ground, he should turn it over so that its crown was downwards—all very like not walking under a ladder and keeping one's fingers crossed.

However, Chinese mining methods were energetic and effective. At the selected spot they dug a rectangular pit (which could be enlarged if ore was found) called an open-cast mine (*lombong*) (Plate 2). A notched tree-trunk served as a ladder to get down into the pit and to climb out of it. On such ladders the miners, like a column of ants, carried up out of the pit baskets full of excavated soil. It might take weeks, even months of digging to get down to the ore, if indeed there was any. In a rainy country the pit filled with water overnight, and so the miners began each day's

2. The method of mining tin prior to 1880, from Scrivenor, 1928.

work by baling out the flood water. Later they used a water-wheel pump, imported from the rice-fields of China (Colour Plate 1).

To bring in a Chinese labour force, and keep it supplied until the export of tin began to repay the outlay, required the investment of substantial sums of money. Malay venturers also had difficulties in controlling an alien labour force, which on one occasion at least rose against them. Later on, the Malay ruling class simply gave concessions to Chinese capitalists who managed their own enter-prises, paying export duty on the tin produced to the local Malay chief at the point of export.

Clearing the jungle caused mosquitoes to breed in vast numbers. It is no surprise that within a year most of the eighty-seven pioneers had died of malaria. But more labourers came to replace them—life was cheap—and on established sites the incidence of malaria was less. By 1860 there was a steady and profitable trade along the river, men and supplies coming in and tin going out, with the river junction the point at which boats were loaded and unloaded. When the tin reached Klang, Raja Abdullah stored it in his warehouse, which still stands, a museum known as the 'Gedong Raja Abdullah', probably the oldest building in the State (*gedung* is the Malay word for 'warehouse').

Two Hakka traders set up a shop at the river junction. It was on the right-hand side of the Klang River (facing upstream) since most of the tracks to the mines started from that bank, so that heavily loaded porters did not have to cross the river on the way to the mines. There was also a track down the valley to Petaling, the next important centre of Chinese mining in that direction. *Kuala* means 'junction' or 'estuary' but in Malay usage it is followed by the name of the river or tributary which ends at that point. Kuala Lumpur should rightly have been called 'Kuala Gombak', but it was not. *Lumpur* can be used as a common noun or adjective to mean 'mud' or 'muddy', but it is rare to find such a construction in idiomatic Malay. One explanation, perhaps a little far-fetched, is that *lumpur* is a corrupt form of a Chinese word meaning 'jungle'. Certain it is that Kuala Lumpur began as a trading post at the river junction. The tracks which ran from it to the mines are to this day preserved in the line of Jalan Ampang, Jalan Pudu, Jalan Petaling, etc. The modern passer-by who goes along these roads can be sure that he follows the weary footsteps of heavily laden porters of 130 years ago.

As the village grew, it took shape around a square. On one side was the river bank, and on the higher ground parallel with the river was the main thoroughfare, known for many years as the High Street (now Jalan Tun H. S. Lee), apparently because it stood on ground above the expected flood level when the river rose. Two shorter lanes ran down from the High Street to the river. They may originally have been 'corrugated' timber paths by which loads were carried to and from the embarkation points on the river. This space, known a little later as Old Market Square, is now Leboh Pasar Besar. Although the buildings and the general appearance may have changed a great deal, these alignments around a rectangle are a relic of the earliest times (Plate 3).

There was a Malay quarter too. The Malays lived apart since the pigs, raised by the Chinese for meat, were offensive to them. The boundary between the Malay quarter and the Chinese settlement around the square was a rough track, later to be called Java Street (and then Mountbatten Road and nowadays Jalan Tun Perak). In the Malay village there was a mosque, with a burial ground on the triangle of land that lay between the Gombak and Klang Rivers (where the Jamek Mosque now stands).

The whole village stood on the east side of the Klang River, for convenient access to mines by tracks leading to Ampang, Batu, and Pudu. On the opposite bank of the river there were some vegetable gardens and a few shanties. But the river, which had no bridges until the 1870s, was a barrier which confined the village to the east side.

From the mid-1860s to 1885 the Chinese headman (Capitan China) of Kuala Lumpur was Yap Ah Loy, one of the many thousands of Chinese peasants who came to South-East Asia in search of a fortune (Plate 4). The migrant worker, far from home, sought security and mutual help (and a decent burial if he died) by association with others of his kind. Thus, it was among the

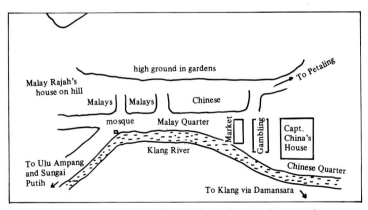

3. Swettenham's sketch map of 1875, the earliest we have, perhaps drawn from memory as he omits the *kuala*, from *Sir Frank Swettenham's Malayan Journals*.

'overseas Chinese' of South-East Asia that the all-pervasive and all-powerful organizations were the so-called 'secret societies'. On arrival in the Straits Settlements the bewildered newcomer (*sinkheh*) was initiated, with ceremonies of blood and drawn weapons intended to frighten him, into membership. He swore total obedience to his society and its leaders, to never to disclose its affairs, and to rally to the aid of any fellow members under attack by their enemies or oppressed by the local authorities. He hoped to find security but was vulnerable to exploitation by his own society, and too easily dragged into gang warfare and riots between rival societies.

Yap Ah Loy was a Hakka Chinese, born in 1837, who first arrived in Malaya in 1854; he never returned to China. In the first years he suffered the adventures and hardships typical of the immigrant labourer. In 1862 he moved to Kuala Lumpur,

4. Yap Ah Loy, Capitan China of Kuala Lumpur for over twenty years, till his death in 1885. (Royal Commonwealth Society Library)

where he was first assistant and, in 1868, successor to the Capitan China. In this position of recognized authority he was also head of the dominant secret society and the largest mining entrepreneur of the district. In his portraits he appears as a short, dour figure with a heavy jaw, obviously a man of determination. It is said that he spoke with a rather gruff voice, but he could also be very jovial. He had that gift which enables a born leader to lift the morale of his followers in times of adversity.

The Selangor civil war which raged from 1867 to 1873 is part of the wider history of Selangor, though its local effects on Kuala Lumpur were devastating. The war was fought between rival coalitions of Bugis and other Malay chiefs, Malay peasants, and Chinese miners, backed by Straits Settlements financiers. In 1872 the Sumatran miners lost confidence in the cause of the Malay viceroy, Tunku Kudin, with whom Yap Ah Loy was allied, and joined his enemies led by three famous warriors, Raja Mahdi, Raja Mahmud and Syed Mashhur, whose names, according to Swettenham, 'were to the western Malay States what that of the Black Douglas was once to Scotland'. Mashhur, who was the most deadly of the three, closed in on Kuala Lumpur, ambushed the European mercenaries of Tunku Kudin and their troops, and burnt the town to the ground. Yap Ah Loy fled through the jungle to Klang, the one remaining town held by Tunku Kudin. But the tide of war turned, and in 1873 Yap Ah Loy came back to the ruins of his town and the surrounding mines, derelict and waterlogged.

In 1874 a British Resident had been sent to Klang to assist Tunku Kudin. Swettenham, the Assistant Resident, came to Kuala Lumpur in March 1875 (he had also been there on a private visit in 1872). He wrote in his journal: 'I went straight to the house of the Captain China ... he offered me champagne, but that I declined, preferring excellent beer which I certainly never expected to find here.' With dynamic energy Yap Ah Loy had already rebuilt the town and Swettenham was much impressed: It was 'by far the best mining village I have seen, the streets wide and excellently arranged, the shops most substantial ... in the front of the Captain's house are the Gambling Booths and the Market ... there are about 1,000 Chinese in the town and some 500 to 700 Malays ... if he had lost heart no one else would have had the courage to stay. If he did not lose heart, he lost money, and it will take him many years of success to recover his lost fortune.'

Just at that time, however, Yap Ah Loy was denied the 'many years of success' which he needed. The mines were only slowly coming back into production. The miners were living precariously on imported supplies obtained on credit from merchants in the Straits Settlements towns. Thus, it was a disaster when the volatile world market price of tin collapsed under the impact of new low-cost production in Australia. The price of tin fell by a third, to its lowest level for thirty years. It was a bleak prospect for Yap Ah Loy, struggling to survive at the end of a long and expensive supply line, paying annual interest on loans at 15 or even 18 per cent. He went on through the years from 1875 to 1878 pleading, cajoling, and cheating his creditors as long as he could, and experimenting with alternatives to mining for tin. By 1878 the British Resident at Klang was predicting that the creditors would finally cut off supplies, bringing Yap Ah Loy to bankruptcy and the mines of Kuala Lumpur to a standstill. But luck, miner's luck, saved Yap Ah Loy as he looked down into the abyss. In 1879 the market turned and the London price of tin rocketed; it rose from £73 to £96 per ton in a single month (October 1879). At last the years of success were upon him. For the rest of his life (he died in 1885) Yap Ah Loy was rich beyond his dreams. It is said that his young sons filched sacks of silver dollars from his counting-house to play ducks and drakes across the rippling waters of the Klang River.

But even success has its price. The boom attracted an influx of new labourers to work on the mines. The population rose by a third in one year and Yap Ah Loy's labour force eventually trebled to more than 4,000. Municipal hygiene had never been a high priority of Yap Ah Loy's regime. If there was money to be made, never mind the muck. In 1875 the streets, compared with other mining villages, seemed 'wide and excellently arranged' but in truth they were narrow lanes, in some instances only 12 feet wide. Into this convenient space the occupiers of adjoining premises threw their rubbish—and there was no one to remove it. Natural disasters such as the flooding of the Klang River and fires which swept through the town took their toll.

The Malay community was an active and busy part of Kuala Lumpur in the 1870s. When the American naturalist William Hornaday visited the town in July 1878 he noted that 'all along the river bank, the houses of the Malays stand in a solid row, on piles 10 feet high, directly over the swift and muddy current'. This was the Sumatran Malay village north of Java Street. As Kuala Lumpur lay within the district of Klang under the control of its Malay chief, he had stationed a small garrison in a stockade on rising ground (in earlier days this was 'Weld Hill', and nowadays is crowned by the towering Maybank building). Yap Ah Loy had lived in amity with the sequence of Malay headmen who occupied the stockade.

The great Malay event of the late 1870s was the visit of Sultan Abdul Samad, the first Malay Ruler to see the town, in May 1879. The Bugis Sultan came in some anxiety (and with a strong guard) lest his Sumatran subjects, remembering ancient emnities, be hostile. But it was an unnecessary concern; the Malays of the interior came in their thousands to pay their loyal respects to this distant, but venerated, potentate, who as a recluse reigned from a capital far away in Kuala Langat. Commercial and political logic dictated that Kuala Lumpur should now be the state capital—and so it became in March 1880.

2
A State Capital in the 1880s

A handful of disconsolate British and Eurasian officials moved in March 1880 from Klang, safe and salubrious, to Kuala Lumpur because higher authority in Singapore had decreed that the flag should follow trade, placing the administrative centre of the State government in the same place as its now thriving commercial hub. No one then knew why an inland area of newly cleared mining lands should be more malarial than Klang with its coastal breezes. But the gravestones in the first Christian cemetery in Venning Road show what happened—and make sad reading. The Resident's daughter died (of cerebral malaria) in her father's arms, while the government apothecary prattled on about trying different medicines.

On first arrival the fear uppermost in their minds was that Yap Ah Loy and his Chinese, resentful of the intrusion upon their domain, would rise and slaughter them. It was not entirely fanciful. There had been episodes of that kind in Sarawak in 1857 and more recently, and nearer home, in 1878 at Pangkor in neighbouring Perak. As they looked around at the menacing wall of jungle surrounding the town, they settled themselves at the greatest possible distance. The 'native town' was on the east bank of the Klang River, and they sited the new 'official quarter' on the other side of the river, and at a distance from it, on the rising ground along which they built Bluff Road (more or less at the back of the Royal Selangor Club where the broad Jalan Sultan Hishamuddin now runs) (Plate 5).

The most energetic advocate of precautions was the Resident himself; he built his Residency on yet higher ground to the north (where the Prime Minister's Office Complex now stands). Here, he installed on his lawn a howitzer gun, giving his visitors demonstrations of the accuracy with which he could lob shells into selected targets in the jungle below. He called it a 'redoubt', which, as Isabella Bird had written of the previous Residency at Klang,

5. The government offices on the rising ground west of the Padang (now Merdeka Square) in the 1890s. The new railway embankment held back the run-off to form an unsightly pool. (Antiques of the Orient)

11

had 'much of the appearance of an armed camp amidst a hostile population'. He need not have worried; Yap Ah Loy now had too much to lose, in his prosperous mines, to risk British reprisals.

As an economy measure, the larger government buildings in Klang had been disassembled so that their component timbers could be shipped upriver and re-erected on these sites in Kuala Lumpur. In these and other activities which did not trouble Yap Ah Loy's business empire the new State capital passed the time until 1882 when the militant Resident, Bloomfield Douglas, was replaced by Swettenham who had known Yap Ah Loy since 1872 and greatly admired his achievements. However, although personal relations were rather better, neither Swettenham nor any of his colleagues spoke Chinese. For years they were blissfully unaware that Yap Ah Loy held sway not by virtue of his empty official title of 'Capitan China' but as 'godfather' of the Chinese secret society dominant in Selangor. They were gratified when he gave them information of the arrival of new secret society headmen, not realizing that he was neatly using their police to crush attempts by rival societies to break into his patch.

But no one could miss the 'pestilential' conditions of filth and disease, and the periodic devastation of the town by fire or flood. Late in 1882 came a task force of buffalo carts and cleaning gangs to remove the accumulated filth (Plate 6). As a longer-term measure it was decided to rebuild the entire Chinese settlement of some 500 houses, replacing mud or wattle walls with baked brick, and palm thatch roofs with tiles. The programme had to be phased over several years (1884–8) to keep demand in line with the flow of building materials. This was done by prescribing a street at a time for complete clearance and rebuilding (with frontages moved back to widen the roads).

Rebuilding was in full swing when the Australian surveyor Ambrose Rathborne found that the streets were littered with bricks and timber. He also gives a vivid account of what had happened in the bad old unreconstructed period: 'On the first alarm of fire, a hurried rush would be made by the inhabitants to close the doors of their shops in order to prevent their contents from being looted. The owners of the wooden houses nearest the conflagration were

6. A bullock cart—used to move goods, rubbish, drinking water, and sick people—though its wheels cut up the roads. (Steven Tan)

busily employed in carrying what they could of their goods to some place of safety. Those in the mud houses simply sat inside and patiently awaited events ... I have seen the roof of a shop catch fire from some spark that had blown on to the thatch unknown to the inmates within, who obstinately refused admittance to those outside endeavouring to enter, so that they might get on to the roof and put out the flames. Shouting and hammering were of no avail, and there was nothing to be done but to break in the door with an axe, when the Chinese occupants were disclosed crouching down and awaiting events with dumb stupidity, seemingly paralyzed by the dread of being robbed should they open their doors and by the fear that the fire after all might reach them.' Yap Ah Loy's fire precautions had been limited to a rule requiring every household to keep a bucket of water standing ready. However, even in the new town, fire continued to be a major hazard, leading to the formation of a volunteer fire brigade, to be described later.

In the market square (Leboh Pasar Besar) there were stalls for which petty traders paid rent to Yap Ah Loy. This was the heart and public forum of Yap Ah Loy's regime, where during the war he had paid silver dollars for the heads of his enemies laid on the table before him, and (according to an official report of 1882) there had been 'a huge gambling booth of jungle rollers roofed with ataps, in which literally all day and all night long, gambling is pursued by a crowd of often excited Chinese and Malays'. It was perhaps as well that Yap Ah Loy, exhausted by thirty years of struggle, died in 1885 at the age of only forty-eight while the long process of adjusting his personal property and public rights—they were indistinguishable—was in its early stages. It was then possible to clear the market square as an open space. A new Central Market was built in Jalan Hang Kasturi; much refurbished as a tourist attraction, it can still be seen.

Yap Ah Loy's successor as Capitan China was his long-time associate, Yap Ah Shak, also a covert secret society boss but a milder man, whose main base was downriver at Petaling. Yap Ah Loy himself became in time a revered but mythical figure of the Chinese pioneer tradition, a mixture of Robin Hood and Prester John described in literature analysed in learned journals. His spendthrift family dissipated his vast wealth and by 1920 were reduced to straightened but respectable circumstances; they still live in Kuala Lumpur.

Governor Weld, visiting Kuala Lumpur in 1886, noted in his official report that it was 'fast becoming the neatest and prettiest Chinese and Malay town ... as within my remembrance it was the dirtiest and most disreputable looking ... picturesque houses and shops brightly painted and often ornamented with carving and gilding form the streets'. Yet it was still an isolated inland centre. When the European residents visited Singapore, their friends sympathized (very difficult to bear) over the hard fate of living in a place in the jungle and knew better than to accept their pressing invitations to pay them a return visit. Isolation was due to the slow and expensive river route; the upstream journey took four days between Klang and Kuala Lumpur. It had nearly ruined Yap Ah Loy in the late 1870s, when the price of tin was too low to cover this extra cost. There was isolation of a different kind in the symbolic barrier between the two halves of the town imposed by the Klang

River, not a majestic stream! The communities lived apart, though in the same town. Much of the story of Kuala Lumpur over the years to 1900 is of practical efforts to surmount these difficulties and to develop the town as a viable entity and a place to enjoy living in. But beneath the 'parish pump' debate about local matters, there is a less obvious change of attitude. In 1886 few would have predicted that Kuala Lumpur would become the leading town of the Malay States; by 1900 no one doubted that it was.

It was necessary to build bridges. In the 1870s there was indeed a crude timber bridge roughly where the Market Street (Leboh Pasar Besar) bridge now stands. The problem was that a bridge constructed of felled jungle trees was of limited width, and so it could not be placed much above the level of the river banks. When the river rose in flood, as it did in December 1881, for example, the force of the flood swept away the bridge. It was no solution to raise the bridge on timber pillars, since the same torrent bringing down trees and other debris would destroy the supports. The ultimate solution, achieved in 1888, was to import iron girders to build a high bridge, with a 90-foot span, at the Market Street crossing.

The first attempt to replace the Klang River as the link with the outside world was a short-lived failure though its traces still survive. In the late 1870s an earth road was built from the village of Damansara, a few miles upstream from Klang, overland to Kuala Lumpur, to cut across the wide southward bend of the river. Where it approached the town it crossed high ground, still known as Damansara Heights (from the Damansara Road), and its final milestone stood in the Brickfields area, which for many years was known to Malays as Batu Limabelas (15th Mile). However, an earth road could never carry the expected volume of goods traffic, moving in bullock carts with metal-rimmed wheels which would cut it up badly. In 1882, before it was complete, a decision was taken to abandon the road and replace it with a railway line.

Like the Damansara Road, the railway project yielded its moments of anguish (Colour Plate 2). In 1886, however, the glad moment arrived for a formal opening of the line to traffic. The Governor, Sir Frederick Weld, came from Singapore to join Sultan Abdul Samad in the inaugural run from Klang to Kuala Lumpur.

A small locomotive had been bought second-hand from Johore, where a railway project had been abandoned, and was named the 'Lady Clarke' (after the wife of the Governor of 1874). A few wooden railway coaches had been built locally; they were rather cramped and stuffy but they would do.

With some apprehension, the 130 passengers climbed abroad. Let the *Straits Times* reporter take up the story. For the first few miles, 'where the line is not yet ballasted', the pace was very deliberate, but there was only 'a slight oscillation'. As they went by, the passengers could see the 'great cutting at Batu Tiga through a troublesome shale formation . . . [and] . . . the places on the line at which subsidences have taken place'. Despite these reminders of obstacles surmounted, 'it was a most comfortable journey throughout', taking some 95 minutes to traverse 20 miles. As the train 'neared Kuala Lumpur the speed was greatly accelerated and we were then going at about 30 miles an hour'. The Sultan, then over eighty years of age, pronounced his first railway journey to be quite the best bullock cart ride he had ever had.

Within three years the railway was yielding an annual surplus of 28 per cent on the capital invested in it. By then, the long process had begun of constructing a line to run from Penang down to Singapore, with an extension to the north-east of Malaya. It went on by fits and starts and the link with Singapore was completed only in 1909 owing to difficulties with the Johore Government about crossing its territory. Until then, a journey from Kuala Lumpur began with the short railway trip to Klang, to embark on a coastal steamer for a 24-hour-voyage (a colourful experience in the early days). In 1890 Sultan Abdul Samad, by now something of a railway buff, went down to Singapore to meet the Duke of Connaught, a son of Queen Victoria, and obtain his consent to naming the new bridge which carried the line from Kuala Lumpur across the river to Klang the Connaught Bridge (and that, in turn, led to the Connaught Bridge power station). Kuala Lumpur, standing at the centre of the growing railway network, became the railway capital, with workshops, etc. which added to its industrial base.

The local extensions of the railway to the outlying mining districts of Selangor cut across the town and entailed a sequence

7. The Straits Trading Company offices, c.1900, to which much tin
   ore was delivered for export, creating a traffic 'black spot'.
   (Antiques of the Orient)

of open level crossings at each of the main north–south streets of
the central area of the town. The more prosperous citizens now
went about town in pony traps, and there were stories, which
gained in the telling, of hair-breadth escapes, by whipping up the
nag to spurt away from the oncoming juggernaut. The railway had

a good safety record, though the 'Lady Clarke' was withdrawn from service in 1893 after an unplanned encounter with another engine coming in the opposite direction. The main hazard was sparks from the engine which set fire to passengers' clothing or goods.

A railway goods yard and engine shed were built on a site north of the modern railway station, and the gates of the goods yard created the first of the town's traffic problems. The *Selangor Journal** tells of 'the risk from a hand-cart coming suddenly out of the gates and wheeling right across the road on to the [Market Street] bridge. Sometimes there are three or four hand-carts on the bridge at one time ... so heavily laden that the man in the shafts has no control either over the cart or over his colleagues in the rear who, with heads bent down, are solely intent on pushing' (Plate 7).

Until road transport on a substantial scale arrived after 1918, the railway was king—the Malay peasant hearing the express whistle as it hurtled past his village called it the 'haughty carriage' (*kereta sombong*)—and Kuala Lumpur was its seat.

*On the *Selangor Journal*, see p. 39 below. The quotations from it are identified in abbreviated form only by the addition of (SJ).

3
A Better Place to Live In

By the 1890s Kuala Lumpur had grown into a sizeable town with a population of about 20,000 comprising several different communities. The improvement of the town, which had gathered momentum in the 1880s, continued apace.

Chinatown, still rather congested, spread along the east bank of the Klang River. Under growing pressure of population, the single-storey buildings were being replaced by what came to be known as 'shophouses', typically of two but sometimes (after 1900) of three storeys. These were a remarkable combination of strictly practical design and artistic embellishment. To make the best use of limited urban space, the individual plots had a narrow street frontage but greater depth. At the front the building owner was required to set back his building to create a covered pavement, called the *kaki lima* because its minimum width was 5 feet. In this way passing pedestrians could walk by under cover from sun and rain and clear of the busy roadway. At his permitted frontage the owner built an open-fronted shop to let in the air, but at the upper level he brought his building forward to project over, and thus cover, the pavement below. The upper storey, or storeys, had shuttered windows to let in light and air, and incidentally to reduce the weight of masonry to be supported above the pavement. The upper rooms were generally used as living accommodation, giving the name 'shophouse', and the storage space was accessible at ground level behind the shop (Colour Plate 3). At the back boundary the owner was required to leave space for a lane, parallel with the street front, which was used by bullock carts collecting nightsoil and, on occasion, by the fire brigade.

The vertical and horizontal features of the design of a typical shophouse front provided space for decoration into which fluted mock pillars with classical 'capitals' and decorative artwork were fitted at all levels. In modern times architectural writers have enthused over 'Chinese Roccoco' and, in later years, art deco influences. But aesthetic appreciation has not—alas—sufficed to preserve very many of the buildings in question. The decorated shophouse, which had its origin in mid-nineteenth century Singapore, is, however, one of the indigenous and eclectic art forms of Kuala Lumpur and other Malayan towns.

The pedestrians did not usually have, as was intended, unimpeded use of the five-foot way. The shopkeeper's goods, such as sacks of rice or other foodstuffs, tended to overflow into this convenient space (Colour Plate 4). Street hawkers, food sellers, proprietors of gaming-tables, or petition writers set up on the pavement. At night livestock were tethered on it. In 1893 a passer-by who had run over a goat in Batu Road (Jalan Raja Laut) counted twenty more goats and two cows 'sleeping in the verandas' at the point where the incident had occurred.

The 'red, blinding, clothes-spoiling dust'—or mud if there had been rain—of the laterite roads was everywhere. Ng Seo Buck recollected that in his boyhood soon after 1900 'prisoners, with chained feet and guarded by an armed policeman, swept the streets early in the morning', and sometimes watered them to lay the dust, but to little effect (Plate 8). Many pedestrians just resigned themselves to it by wearing drab, khaki clothes, less likely to show the stains. Along the streets passed the pony traps of the well-to-do, the gharries plying for hire, and most numerous of all the rickshaws, the poor man's taxi, with a puller toiling between the shafts. At night the streets were illuminated by flickering kerosene oil-lamps on wooden poles; these had only recently replaced lamps fuelled with coconut oil.

The red dust and the pot-holes in the roads were due to the crumbling of the laterite roads under the dense traffic of the town centre, particularly the heavily laden bullock carts coming in from the mines or bringing supplies to the shops. In 1890 repair work was confined to semi-naked Indian labourers apathetically filling pot-holes. Better methods improved the surface without laying the dust. It was only with tarmac, to meet the needs of mass road transport, after the war, that a solution was found.

The town on the east bank was steadily extending its boundaries,

8. A street maintenance gang, possibly convicts under guard by a
   warder (*second from left*). (Steven Tan)

mainly southwards, with reclamation of swamps, construction of
additional girder bridges, etc. With larger-scale building operations
came a demand for materials, for which a 'Government Factory'
was built in the Brickfields district; Jalan Tun Sambanthan, which is
the main thoroughfare, was until recently known as Brickfields Road.
This was also the main centre of the Ceylonese community, who
in 1894 built a Buddhist temple in what is now Jalan Berhala.

Old Sultan Abdul Samad was pressed by his British officials to
make Kuala Lumpur his principal seat, to lend it the prestige of
being a royal capital, but the wily old Ruler much preferred his
rural retreat at Jugra in the Kuala Langat district. Characteristically,
he avoided an outright refusal and played for time. Jalan Sultan
probably owes its name to its proximity to rising ground, on which
a site for a royal residence was cleared. The Sultan's grandson, and
eventual successor, Raja Muda Sulaiman, designed a splendid complex with a walled enclosure in which there would be a flagstaff,
royal lodgings and offices, accommodation for visiting dignitaries
(allocated between rajas, sons of rajas, lesser Malay notables, and

21

European visitors, all according to their standing), but it was never built. The old Sultan died in peace at Jugra in 1898, and his successor decided to make his residence at Klang, at a distance from the polyglot metropolis of Kuala Lumpur.

The original Malay quarter, with its market, mosque, and school, along the river bank north of Java Street, preserved its character—with Malay Street, Malacca Street, and Johore Street—but lacked space for expansion. This led to the creation, in 1902, of a new settlement (Kampung Bahru) further north. It was a well-intentioned project which aspired to promote traditional Malay industries in a new urban context. That part of the scheme did not thrive but Kampung Bahru itself, with its village garden atmosphere, became a continuing part of the growing town, a new residential area for the increasing Malay population, including government employees (Colour Plate 5).

The small but mixed Indian community had no recognized 'quarter'. Its main focus was perhaps the Sri Maha Mariamman Temple in the High Street (Jalan Tun H. S. Lee) founded by Thambusamy Pillai, whose career is described in a later chapter. On the edge of the original Malay quarter, away from the river, a number of Chettiars (moneylenders from a South Indian caste) set up their businesses.

By the 1890s the more prosperous members of all communities had begun to live outside the town as it was crowded, noisy, and sometimes smelly. The richest Chinese towkays, such as Chow Ah Yeok, the leading Cantonese, built impressive residences, for show as much as occupation—there were sometimes more compact annexes for living in—along the road to Ampang (Jalan Ampang). To the north of the town (Jalan Raja Laut—then Batu Road) stood the houses of a more mixed group of notables, which included Raja Muda Sulaiman, Thambusamy Pillai, Loke Yew, and some European businessmen, such as Henry Huttenbach and J. C. Pasqual. These houses, built for display, were ideal media for the elaborate decorative style which had its modest beginnings in the shophouse. Fortunately, one of the finest of them, the Wisma Loke, built in 1904 for the millionaire Loke Yew, has been preserved as an art gallery and music conservatory. It originally stood in

22

9. A football match on the Padang (Merdeka Square) in July 1903. Note the various vehicles and the child. (Foreign and Commonwealth Office Library)

splendour in an 11-acre estate and its features include Renaissance arcades and a traditional Chinese entry gate. The last of these show houses, in a rather simpler style, was built in 1929. This was Bok House, the pride of Chua Cheng Bok who had made his fortune by importing motor cars. It is now a restaurant standing on Jalan Ampang.

For the European community, the Police Parade Ground (Merdeka Square) was the centre of social life. Here, in the course of the 1890s, were built the Selangor Club, St Mary's Church, the Chartered Bank building, and the new government offices (Bangunan Sultan Abdul Samad). It was no longer just a police parade-ground. Under the influence of enthusiastic sportsmen, it became a playing-field for cricket and other team games, and was made into a level sward and called 'the Padang' (Plate 9).

In 1888 Alfred Venning, one of the European officials who identified himself so much with Kuala Lumpur that he is prominent in its story, began to lay out a botanic garden (Venning had originally been a planter in Ceylon) (Plate 10). This was the beginning of the Lake Gardens, perhaps the finest amenity bequeathed by the pioneers to the modern citizens of the city. With a great deal of support and help from colleagues and from local figures such as Chow Ah Yeok, whose initial contribution was a hundred white chempaka and orange trees, Venning developed almost 200 acres of wasteland into a public park, with a chain of small lakes as its central feature (Plate 11). Around this prestigious and attractive area roads were built and, in time, official residences sited on the higher ground. Modern times have added the Parliament Building and the National Monument (to the Malayan Armed Forces).

In 1889, however, public health, or rather epidemic disease, required priority attention. There was a small hospital, with an out-patient department, among the government buildings on Bluff Road but it barely sufficed for the needs of the town population, particularly the government staff, and it could do little for the thousands of Chinese working on the mines in conditions which were bound to spread disease.

On the mines when a labourer fell sick he took to his bed, such as it was, and hoped to recover. In Kuala Lumpur Yap Ah Loy had

10. (a) Sultan Abdul Samad; (b) Loke Yew; (c) Thambusamy Pillai; and (d) Alfred Venning.

11. The Lake Gardens, c.1890, a favourite subject for photography.
(Antiques of the Orient)

maintained a traditional Chinese death-house to which men were
brought in their last hours. In the 1880s slow-moving bullock carts
brought in to Kuala Lumpur dying coolies who, since they could
not and their employers would not, pay hospital charges, were
taken to the 'pauper ward' of the hospital, where one in four died
within twenty-four hours of admission. Reporting in 1888,
Swettenham gave a grim picture of 'hospitals terribly overcrowded,
40,000 Chinese immigrants introduced to a most trying climate
and hard work where only the fittest survive'.

A new Pauper (i.e. 'free') Hospital was built on the outskirts of
the town, on the site of the modern Kuala Lumpur Hospital
(formerly, General Hospital). A sort of by-pass, Circular Road
(now Jalan Tun Razak), was built to the east of the town so that

bullock carts approaching from the outlying mines could reach the new hospital without having to pass through the congested streets of the town centre. The new system was a great improvement but ran into new problems. If the sick men began to recover, they immediately tried to escape from this uncongenial institution, so that it was necessary to surround it with a high fence.

The Malays and Chinese of all walks of life had a deep distrust of European hospitals. The Malays argued that since so many patients died in hospital, the doctors must be poisoning them to avoid the shame of admitting that they could not cure them. The visitors' book of the Pauper Hospital was found to contain an entry denouncing 'a red-haired Frenchman, a cruel-hearted man, who delighted in blood' (in fact, he was a Danish surgeon with dark hair). The Chinese community raised the money with which to build their own T'ung Shin Hospital on Jalan Pudu, staffed by Chinese doctors and managed by a Chinese board of management. In their official reports, the European medicos showed a friendly interest in 'the rival firm', noting that it used homoeopathic 'decoctions of herbs or roots', prescribed for each patient according to his individual needs and stored in 'scores of small earthen kettles labelled with the tickets of the respective patients'.

At last, in 1893, the time had come and the resources were available to build a new and prestigious government office block, on a different site closer to the town centre, on the vacant east side of the Padang (Plate 12). After some dissension with the Government Architect whose taste was for the English town hall classical style modelled on Greek temples, the style chosen for the new building was the 'Muhammadan' or 'Neo-saracenic', developed in India, which combined some features of Indian Muslim architecture with Gothic and other European elements. It was certainly something quite new in Malaya. The resulting structure, now the Bangunan Sultan Abdul Samad, was completed in 1897, on time and within the estimated cost (Plate 13). The wiseacres had predicted that the building, or at least its tall clock tower, would collapse. The design was done by a young man named Bidwell, a brilliant architect who, disgruntled at the credit diplomatically given to the Government Architect, A. C. Norman (whose name appears on the foundation

12. The government offices (Bangunan Sultan Abdul Samad), with cricket on the Padang, *c*.1903. (Steven Tan)

stone), went on to become the leader of his profession in Singapore. The engineers modified and strengthened the foundations and lower range of his building as they perceived the need in the course of building it. This product of talent and trial and error still stands a century later despite the excavation of the space in front (Merdeka Square) to accommodate an underground car park.

It has its legends: there was no serious accident to any of the artisans who built it, and its 4 million bricks were thrown up, two at a time, without even one being dropped. Local residents had for years complained that 'the horrible 12 o'clock gun literally shakes our house' and that its reverberation would bring down the clock tower (SJ). (The gun was fired by the police in Bluff Road as a time signal to the town to set its clocks by.) But it did not, though the number of times it was fired each day was reduced.

To the opening ceremony came senior figures—and journalists—from Singapore. For the inaugural ball the interior was decorated and lit by electricity (the town did not get a regular electricity supply for another ten years). The exterior was 'floodlit' by gas burners. The visitors came to mock but returned home somewhat abashed at the finest building in the Malay States. Thereafter, a number of other major new buildings—the town hall, the post

13. The government offices from across the river, taken in 1897 before the clock had been installed. (Antiques of the Orient)

office, and, in 1911 after years of delay, the third railway station (which still stands)—were built in the same original and attractive style.

In 1890 Kuala Lumpur had neither a piped water supply nor a drainage and refuse disposal system. Some householders drew their water from wells of doubtful purity. Water drawn from the river upstream of the town was brought by bullock cart to storage tanks at the market, so that this main centre of food distribution could be washed down. Here there was a municipal bathhouse for both sexes. None the less, there were some appalling black spots. An inspection report on the three bakeries in 1890 stated that one resembled a pigsty rather than a bakery and that its water came from a well *believed* to be untainted by the surrounding filth. In the early 1890s, however, Kuala Lumpur got a much improved water supply by the construction of a large catchment reservoir in the hills above the town. It took many years to complete the distribution reservoirs and the pipes to individual houses. Even in 1902 most streets had their stand-pipes from which the inhabitants drew their daily supply of water.

Bullock carts were everywhere and somewhere had to be found in which the bullocks could be stabled for the night. To this day, an area in the Brickfields district is known as Kandang Kerbau (cattle pound). It was originally an open space on which bullock cart owners built stables, to an approved standard plan. Keeping livestock in the centre of the town was then prohibited (not with universal success, however). In the garden suburbs, however, the residents were permitted to build stables for the ponies which pulled their carriages.

Money was found for improving the general appearance of the town. Vacant land at street junctions was planted with bushes, etc. and flowering trees edged the outer streets of the town. When Ethel Douglas Hume first arrived in 1899, her brother drove her to his house through the Lake Gardens: 'We bowled over perfect roads, past rounded hills with sloping swards, past fantastic palms and stretches of lily-covered water, where wreaths of mist shimmered steely grey in the starlight. "Joseph," I whispered, "this is fairyland." '

4
The People of Kuala Lumpur

THE 'new comrade' (*sinkheh*) may have been tempted from China by reports that Malayan streets were paved with gold, but even before he had discovered that more prosaic materials were in use, he had had some bruising experiences. He had left behind for years, perhaps for ever, the stability of his native village, with its network of kinship and predictable customs. The voyage to Singapore was uncomfortable. The fourteen-year-old Choo Kia Peng was one of 1,300 deck passengers who sailed from Swatow in 1895 on a vessel of 3,000 tons. The smell of fresh garlic stacked on deck 'nearly drove me mad', and when the ship ran into a typhoon 'a huge wave came over us and carried me and another passenger to the edge of the ship ... I was as sick as a rat'. Arriving at Singapore the immigrant flotsam and jetsam passed through incomprehensible checks and formalities, and were marched to and from a transit depot under the escort of 'coolie brokers' determined to prevent any of their human cargo from absconding or being nabbed by competitors. After the journey on by coastal steamer and railway train to Kuala Lumpur, the new arrival, unless he had friends to receive him, was put into the official Immigration Depot (at the end of Jalan Petaling) until released into employment under a written contract which gave him rights, in so far as he could insist on them, but required him to repay the cost of his passage by working for the employer for a fixed period (Colour Plate 6).

The job itself, whatever it was, required long hours of often back-breaking labour in a climate more enervating than that of South China. As in Yap Ah Loy's time, the immigrant labourer sought companionship and protection among others of the same dialect group and district of China, though 'secret societies' were now banned (but by no means suppressed). He was one of a Chinese working population of men aged in most cases between

31

twenty and fifty with a ratio (in 1901) of ten men to every woman. His only brief contact with a woman of his community would be in one of the brothels—Kuala Lumpur had thirty-nine registered brothels in 1890 in which some 500 women, mainly Chinese, plied their unhappy trade in cramped cubicles with little ventilation. Unless the urban worker lived on the job, such as a shop assistant sleeping amid the odours of his employer's stock-in-trade, or slept rough on a covered pavement, he had his base in a crowded lodging-house, where the men slept in wooden beds fixed to the walls in tiers, on canvas or straw cots in the centre of the room, and on the floor in the passageway. In some cases the man had no more than the shared use of a bed for twelve or even eight hours, so that it might be hired to someone else during his working shift. Here he kept his box with his few possessions, often including an opium pipe (Colour Plate 7).

The last Capitan China of Selangor, the recognized head of the community, was Yap Kwan Seng, who held office from 1889 to 1901. He was an affable, sociable man, whose official residence was the formal seat of his authority (Plate 14). Here, there was a hall of audience in which he sat to arbitrate on disputes or consult on matters of public concern. He was one of the commercial magnates who sat on the State Council, the Sanitary Board (town council), and the committees which managed the immigration depot and the Chinese hospital. Between them and the mass of the working-class Chinese were the smaller capitalists, shopkeepers, traders, mining employers, etc.

The local festivals yielded some striking contrasts. At Chinese New Year in 1895 Jalan Petaling was 'lined on each side by stalls; crowded in every conceivable crook and cranny by Chinese; two continuous lines of carriages, gharries and rikishas—one young Chinese "blood" had a carriage and six with outriders—going in either direction; Chinese "bands" playing in the first floor of seemingly every house; a glaring sun, a blinding dust, and a strong odour of cooking, etc. floating around' (Plate 15). The pomp was sometimes almost regal. When, for example, Chow Ah Yeok, leader of the Cantonese community, died in 1892, the same source tells us that there was a 'lying in state' in which those who came to pay

14. The town residence (in Jalan Pudu) of the last Capitan China, drawing by R. D. Jackson, *c*.1910. (J. A. Nicholson)

their respects could admire 'a magnificent pall of blue silk richly embroidered with gold' covering the coffin. At a less pretentious level, when a towkay built a new house the 'excellent and artistic workmanship' of the traditional decorative features were a source of pride (SJ).

Until the 1890s the Malays of Kuala Lumpur had been Sumatran

33

15. Petaling Street on a quiet day; the processional route of Chinese feast days, drawing by R. D. Jackson, *c.*1910. (J. A. Nicholson)

traders. This element persisted, though they now found the out-lying rural areas more congenial than Kuala Lumpur itself. One of the members of this class was Haji Mohamed Taib who came to Kuala Lumpur in 1876 from Menangkabau and prospered exceed-ingly until his death in 1925. He became one of the richest Malays in Selangor, owning tin-mines, plantation land, and large numbers

34

of houses and shops in Malay Street and the environs of Kuala Lumpur. The new class of Malay government employees, a varied group, provided a mixed element in the main body of the Malay community. The police and their families numbered about a thousand, and there were smaller numbers in other services. Non-commissioned police officers were respected figures in Malay society. However, the leadership of the Kuala Lumpur Malays passed to a few members of the ruling dynasty, who left the traditional base of their class in the coastal districts, to assert their status in a new field.

For many years, until his death in 1913, the recognized Malay grandee of Kuala Lumpur was Raja Laut, a son of a previous Sultan, and under the new regime a member of the State Council, the Sanitary Board (town council), Malay Magistrate, and headman (*penghulu*) of Kuala Lumpur. Raja Laut appeared to be absorbed in the contemplation of his own noble rank and the inferiority of those about him. That was perhaps a rather harsh official comment on his stately and perfunctory performance of his duties as a government official. Raja Laut's forte was flowery public oratory in giving public addresses on ceremonial occasions, such as the visit of a Governor or the departure of a Resident on transfer to another post. Thus, when Governor Weld arrived to open the railway in 1886, the *Straits Times* reported Raja Laut was in full oratical flow—'previous to the British government ... we felt like one wandering in the jungle, our way beset by thorns and thickets ...', etc. On the accession in 1898 of Sultan Sulaiman, who had no grown-up sons, Raja Laut was elevated to the office of Raja Muda vacated by the new Ruler.

On the death of Raja Laut, his role in Kuala Lumpur devolved on Raja Bot, another minor 'royal' but a more Westernized dignitary; he once, during a smallpox epidemic, gave a useful lead in organizing a vaccination clinic for his countrymen, who were very dubious about this medical technique. Raja Bot's speciality was court ceremonial, which he elaborated to an unprecedented degree for the new Ruler. He was an inveterate gambler who slipped away to Singapore to have an unobtrusive flutter.

Even at this stage there were survivors of the Malay fighting captains who had been the terror of the State around 1870. Raja Mahdi himself had died in exile in 1882, but Syed Mashhur had eventually returned to become *penghulu* of Kerling in Ulu Selangor. When he left his rural retreat to come into town, men stepped down from the five-foot way into the road to avoid jostling a man who was remembered (he had destroyed Kuala Lumpur in 1872) as the 'fastest gun' in Selangor. Raja Mahmud had a similar reputation; Hugh Clifford wrote that he claimed to have 'slain two hundred men—not counting Chinamen'. After a rather chequered career in Selangor in the 1880s he eventually returned from exile to enliven the official celebrations of the end of the Anglo–Boer War in 1902 with an electrifying demonstration of hand-to-hand duelling with the kris, reported in the *Malay Mail*—'now advancing, now retreating, with one foot gracefully poised, hands working and eyes always watchful'.

In 1892 Sultan Abdul Samad made one of his infrequent visits to join with the Governor in opening a railway extension (see Plate 10). He was now almost ninety, but came by train. 'As His Highness stept out of the railway carriage, the big gun from the barracks on the hill fired a salute, the Guard of Honour presented arms, and the Band played the Selangor March. Some 70 followers came with the Sultan, one in particular carrying the sword of honour presented by the Queen, immediately behind him. As the old man, struggling with his "baju" [he disliked wearing it and put it on at the last moment], walked slowly past ... the scene made one realise the fact, which one is sometimes apt to forget here, that this is after all a Malay State with a Malay Sultan at its head' (SJ).

In the Indian community, as in the Chinese, prominent and influential citizens owed their position to wealth and commercial success. There was not as yet a large number of Indian labourers— they were drawn in by the rapid expansion of the rubber industry after 1905. The Indian mercantile group was much smaller than the Chinese. The majority of the Indians in Selangor were Hindus from South India, though the police recruited Sikhs and Punjabi Muslims (sometimes called 'Pathans' in the records of the time). The paramilitary Malay States Guides (formed in 1896) was entirely

North Indian. After completing their service, Sikhs sometimes remained as night-watchmen, moneylenders, etc. The Sinhalese clerical class was often, to its disgust, lumped with the Ceylon Tamil element, and mention has already been made of the small but important group of Chettiar moneylenders, also from South India.

Among the Indians the leading figure was Thambusamy Pillai, who had first come to Selangor in 1875 as a clerk in the newly formed Resident's office at Klang (see Plate 10). The government service did not satisfy his aspirations, however, and in 1889 he resigned to begin a new, and very profitable, career as tin miner, moneylender, and government contractor. More than any of his Asian contemporaries, he could build bridges; according to Robson, he 'knew everybody and was known to everybody ... a leading light at the Selangor club ... almost an institution in himself ... keenly interested in racing ... a curry tiffin at his house on the Batu Road was something to remember ...'. His main legacy to his own community was the Sri Maha Mariamman Temple which, for twenty years after his death in 1902, was almost a family possession, though this gave rise to a bitter dispute among the Indian community in 1924.

The European community was predominantly official, though by the 1890s the unofficial element was increasing. There were a few among them who had a real concern for the improvement of the town. Enough has been said of Venning. Another was the public works engineer, H. F. Bellamy. Bellamy's real enthusiasm was reserved for the volunteer fire brigade, which he raised and led. In time, the brigade acquired a pair of shire-horses to pull the wagon with the water tank and crew. Bellamy would mount the box and drive his team through the streets to the fires to the astonishment (at the huge horses) of the populace.

European life was dominated by status—'a doosid lot of side', said one embittered new arrival to the *Selangor Journal*. Its focus was the clubs, where they played and spent convivial evenings. Ethel Hume who arrived in such ecstasy (see p. 30 above) summed up the social round as 'from five to six you drive, leave cards, play golf, tennis, or croquet, and then it is suddenly dark ... you may appear in a crumpled state at the Club, and play cards or study the papers under a punkah. Dinner is a late function generally. . . .'

The mock Tudor design of the Selangor Club was the work of Arthur Norman of the Public Works Department, who had qualified as an architect in Devon before coming to Selangor in 1883 (Plate 16). He had previously worked around Plymouth on the restoration of genuine Tudor houses and Gothic country churches. The latter expertise helped him in designing St Mary's Church.

The Selangor Club was generally known as 'the Spotted Dog', and the most credible explanation of the name is that it was open to members of all communities, though the Malay and Chinese members, unlike the sociable Thambusamy Pillai, did not use the club very much—it was not their kind of institution. But in the 1890s it was a mixed club at which Venning, the State Treasurer, played billiards with his chief clerk. The atmosphere was, however, already changing. The senior members of the European community, the *tuan besar*, were unenthusiastic about resorting to the same club as the lesser European mortals whom they met in their working lives. Hence it was that in 1890 a group of them, without

16. The Selangor Club, built in 1890 in timbered mock Tudor style. (Steven Tan)

1. Old mining pits abandoned and flooded, water-colour by Mary Barnard, c.1910, from Harrison, 1923.

2. Governor Weld cutting the first sod at Kuala Lumpur, in July 1883, to begin laying the railway to Klang, from *The Graphic*, 3 November 1883. (Antiques of the Orient)

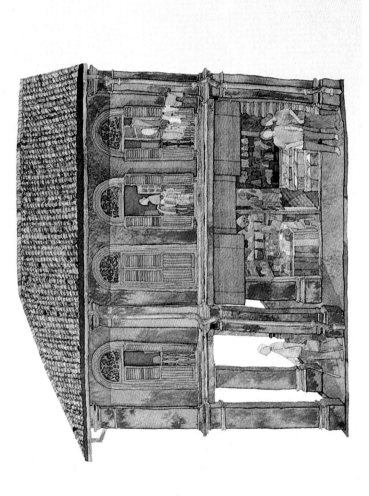

3. A traditional two-storey shophouse front showing commercial and domestic uses, c.1910–20, water-colour by Victor Chin, 1993. (Victor Chin)

4. A blind basket seller and food hawker at a street corner, water-colour by
    Dorothea Aldworth, *c.*1910, from Coote, 1923.

5. Batu Road near Kampung Bahru, water-colour by Kathleen Russell, 1932. (T. B. Russell)

6. A Chinese lantern shop, one of the many trades of Kuala Lumpur, water-colour by Dorothea Aldworth, *c.*1910, from Coote, 1923.

7. A rickshaw—'the poor man's taxi'—less overcrowded than usual. (Steven Tan)

8. The Mak Inang, a modern dance in traditional style, water-colour by Mohamed Hoessin bin Enas, from *Malaysians*, 1963. (Shell Companies in Malaysia)

9. Chinese *wayang* or theatre, water-colour by Mohamed Hoessin bin Enas, from *Malaysians*, 1963. (Shell Companies in Malaysia)

10. The Looi temple on Jalan Ampang, water-colour by Kathleen Gemmill, 1963. (T. B. Russell)

11. The Jamek Mosque (1909) at the *kuala* (river junction); for many years it was the principal town mosque.

12. The Town Hall and Municipal Building (1903).

13. The Railway Station (1911).

14. A rubber tapper at work—a delicate operation, water-colour by Mohamed Hoessin bin Enas, from *Malaysians*, 1963. (Shell Companies in Malaysia)

15. Old Market Square (Leboh Pasar Besar), c.1920, when cars were in common use. (Steven Tan)

16. A panoramic view of modern Kuala Lumpur with St Mary's Church in the foreground. (Revd C. K. Samuel)

breaking away entirely from the Selangor Club, formed their own club, the Lake Club, in the Lake Gardens, with rates of subscription set to discourage applications from less well-paid colleagues.

The first printing press was brought to Kuala Lumpur in 1890. Until then, official documents had been printed on a limited scale in Singapore. From 1890 the Government Printer published the *Selangor Government Gazette* in fortnightly issues. The press had spare capacity, and in 1892 began to publish the *Selangor Journal*, a magazine and local newsletter which also appeared at fortnightly intervals. It was edited by the Government Printer, John Russell, whose observant eye and quiet humour make it fascinating reading, a chronicle of the times (admittedly very Eurocentric, but not exclusively so). Russell had helpers, one of whom was John Robson, who had become an administrator in Selangor in 1889 after a brief apprenticeship as a planter in Ceylon.

Robson was to spend most of the rest of his life in Kuala Lumpur (he died in internment in Singapore in 1945), as a businessman, public figure, and commentator on matters of interest, with a particularly sympathetic eye for the advancement of the Malays. In 1896 he borrowed some money from his friends, including Loke Yew, who was to be the leader of the Chinese business community for the next twenty years (he died in 1917). Robson, then aged twenty-six, resigned from the government service and used the loan to set up the first Selangor newspaper, the *Malay Mail*, purchasing from a defunct Singapore newspaper a primitive flat bed printing press. With the aid of one Ceylonese clerk, Robson, working from a shophouse in Java Street, produced a sixteen-page daily with an initial print run of 200 copies. He was his own editor, manager, advertising manager, and printer. In his memoirs he recalled how, after hours spent in setting the type and arranging the pages, the sheets (of four pages each) were fed by hand into the printing and folding machinery. His farewell comment was that 'if I had my time over again I should have no desire whatever to start a daily newspaper in Malaya or elsewhere'. But Kuala Lumpur should be grateful that he did. With the advent of the *Malay Mail*, the *Selangor Journal* had served its purpose and was discontinued—a sad loss to us.

5
Fun and Games

EACH community in Kuala Lumpur had its recreations, typically the celebration of festivals, such as the end of the Fasting Month for Malays, Chinese New Year, Hindu occasions like Deepavali or Thaipusam, and Christmas for the Europeans. Of more interest perhaps were activities such as playing games, which in time built bridges across the intercommunal divides.

In towns such as Kuala Lumpur dramatic performances, with their colourful costumes, music and rhythm, and skilful dancing, were a prime entertainment for the working-class of all Asian communities (Colour Plate 8). The plot sometimes drew on traditional tales but was augmented by topical allusions. Professional performers, usually touring companies, earned their living by providing what their audience wanted. A Malay scholar like Wilkinson might describe the Malay *bangsawan* as 'a tawdry show', vulgar and full of foreign elements, but, like the English pantomime, which it somewhat resembled, it was splendid fun.

By the end of the nineteenth century the *bangsawan*, originally performed in Penang by Indian actors in the 1870s, had become the leading *urban* form of Malay drama. Robson, as his own drama critic, went to a performance in Kuala Lumpur in 1903 given by Malay actors. It purported to depict the gory story of Bluebeard (a legendary English wife-killer); he noted it was enlivened at one point with singing in Malay the current English drawing-room ballad 'And Her Golden Hair'. The story really did not matter; by convention its leading figures were vaguely aristocratic. But if the 'principal boy' (Orang Muda) and the 'principal girl' (Seri Panggung) were crossed in love, that could be expressed in song and dance, and interrupted by the antics of comedians.

The Chinese theatre was no less colourful and almost as eclectic (Colour Plate 9). As early as 1880 Governor Weld, in a diary entry of a visit to Kuala Lumpur, described a performance: 'It was allegorical, and represented all the Rajahs, headed by the Sultan, giving up their quarrels and putting themselves under the Governor's protection . . . afterwards they sang an ode of welcome . . . I can't describe the gorgeousness of the principal personages . . . with their banners and dressed in the most brilliant colours, and rich materials, stiff with embroideries, i.e. gold and silver . . . then there were tumblers executing antics in scarlet trousers and blue jackets.'

Weld 'was glad to leave as soon as the part addressed to me was over, and got to bed about 12 p.m. after a very hard day's work'. Twenty years later, when Ng Seo Buck was a boy, there were 'vermin-stricken halls in which Cantonese Wayang played year in year out'. More significant is the opposition of Chinese mining employers to applications for licences to open a theatre; they argued that it increased absenteeism among their labourers, for whom such performances were a touch of colour in drab, monotonous working lives.

Let us turn to games which had a more widespread appeal. No one knows when soccer was first played in Malaya, though the *Singapore Free Press* reported a gathering on New Year's Day 1849 to kick a ball about as 'an exciting game of football, in which all joined'. Its impact on Selangor from about 1890 was dramatic. This was the time when it was found that the sure recipe for a well-attended Malay village school (not easily achieved in the climate of kampong opinion of the time) was to equip it with a football pitch (and to provide—as an inducement to pious parents—that a Muslim religious teacher was on hand to give afternoon lessons in the faith).

To begin with, Europeans poked fun at adult Malay footballers in Kuala Lumpur. The *Selangor Journal* wrote that 'The natural gravity and dignity of the Malay is easily noticeable. No preliminary horseplay or turning of somersaults as amongst English school-boys can be seen. After a lot of talking, which is shared equally by all the players, the ball is started. The game reminds one of the descriptions one reads of ladies' football matches in England. The players make apologetic charges and stand around in picturesque attitudes. The full back may be seen stretched at full length smoking a cigarette whilst a mildly fierce battle is being waged near his opponents' goal. Should the ball happen to trickle his way he will come to life and spread hiself around gracefully until the tide of conflict has once more rolled backwards. The costumes worn by the players are very "chic".'

But the attitude soon changed to a fierce will to win. By 1912 the Selangor Football Association had three Malay teams in a total of eight. When one of the Malay teams was playing, its supporters lined the touch-line with shouts of *bunuh* (kill) and *tendang* (strike).

The other great attraction, which was a social as much as a sporting event, was horse-racing (Plate 17). The Selangor Gymkhana Club was formed in 1890, and it immediately attracted the support of prominent Chinese, some as owners, all as punters. In the early years there were no professional jockeys and those Europeans who were good horsemen, notably Harry Syers, head of the police, rode in the races. Serious events were interspersed with comic turns such as mounting while holding an open umbrella and lighting a cigar and keeping it alight to the finishing line.

It soon became more professional. The Selangor Turf Club replaced the Gymkhana Club and the ban on jockeys was lifted; many, like the horses, came from Australia. The key figure of the

17. The racecourse at Kuala Lumpur, *c.*1900. (Steven Tan)

Malayan racing fraternity was a retired jockey, 'Daddy Abrams', 'an exceedingly good judge of a horse and a shrewd businessman, withal a most genial character . . . the leading horse-dealer and trainer'. This picture is taken from a history of Singapore which was his base, but he had been known to ride, at 13½ stone, as far afield as Sungei Ujong. There is no record that he ever came to Kuala Lumpur though he supplied many of its racehorses.

When Edith Stratton Brown arrived in 1896 to become head-mistress of the new girls' school, she found that a Kuala Lumpur race meeting was 'like a big family party. There was a native stand a short distance away from the club stand. Malay royalty and heads of the Chinese and Indian communities, came to the European side being members of the club and owners of race horses. . . . Ladies did not do their own betting. A steward, one of the British members, always came up to the Ladies' Gallery and asked if they would like to buy a ticket. The Chartered Bank closed on Race Days and took all their clerks, etc. to the Turf Club and ran the betting part . . . tea with ice cream was served. Ices were always made in those days in portable tubs specially made to contain freezing ingredients. At 5 p.m. when the last race was run people strolled about the Padang to get good views of all the dresses.' To round off a race meeting, the Resident often gave a ball.

Golf, at this period, had a less universal appeal. The history of the Selangor Golf Club recalls that the first course of the [Royal] Selangor Golf Club was an old Chinese burial ground on Petaling Hill (the present site of the Victoria Institution). 'A human skull . . . might be dislodged by a player who wandered into remote corners and sought to extricate himself by the firm, rather than scientific, use of a niblick.' The first Asian players were the caddies, who were all Malays since the Chinese would not resort to such haunted ground. They 'would themselves, on the day of their competition, prepare a Malay curry tiffin for the members they served in conjunction with the clubhouse boys, after which they went out to do battle'. The members kept the caddies' scorecards and adjudicated on the observance of the rules; 'there was often a good deal of betting on the results of these competitions in the old days and it has been known for members' arithmetic to be suspect when one of his men won.' The first Asian member of the golf club is said to have been Choo Kia Peng, who was the leading Selangor Chinese between the wars, a very sociable man—a prominent rotarian, for example—but a non-playing member.

There were quieter and more orderly pleasures. In March 1896 'Mr Danbury, from Singapore, gave entertainments with a phonograph; the rain on each afternoon, however, prevented a large attendance of visitors'. There was wider appeal in proposals for the erection of bandstands in the Lake Gardens and on the Padang. When the Sanitary Board discussed this interesting suggestion, the Capitan China and Loke Yew 'very generously offered to find the necessary sum for erecting a temporary stand on the Parade Ground'. Public performances were given twice a week by the police band (SJ).

This was an era, before mechanical music making, when everyone was expected to take his or her 'harp to the party' to entertain the company. At the European clubs there were 'smoking concerts', where the men could indulge in what was still a masculine taste and the range of entertainment was correspondingly of 'stag party' type. Robson tells how two frustrated females hid under the Selangor Club, raised on stilts, to listen to what went on. They so much enjoyed the humour that their laughter gave them away, and they were invited in. That was the end of exclusively male gatherings.

Occasionally, someone came to Kuala Lumpur from the wider world to issue a challenge. One such was Mr Hancock, who described himself as a 'champion walkist'. In 1894 he offered to race over 4 miles against a local team of eight, each of whom would, in relay, compete against him for only half a mile. He beat the local team—six Sikhs from the police and two Europeans.

The same year introduced Kuala Lumpur to aviation in the person of a hot air balloonist who offered to make an ascent: 'Everything being declared in readiness, the "Practical Aeronaut and Aerial Engineer" again addressed the throng, informing them that, although not enough money had been subscribed to cover expenses (to say nothing of the damage to the Club grounds; a point, however, which he did not mention), he was about to risk his life, and that he hoped that if he was successful something hand-some would be done for him. He then moved off to the parachute, while a local sportsman dashed through the crowd with a bottle of beer wherewith to refresh him, took leave of his colleagues, bade farewell to his wife, ordered the stays to be cast off, and, amidst enthusiastic clapping and cheering slowly soared aloft to a height of twenty feet' (SJ).

Formal ceremonies, such as police or military parades, were certain to draw a crowd. The local high noon of empire was per-haps the celebration in 1897 of Queen Victoria's Diamond Jubilee, which is reported at much length in the *Selangor Journal* (Plate 18). Notables of all communities served on organizing committees for collecting subscriptions and arranging processions, illuminations, fireworks, decorations, and sports. Subcommittees dealt with the bullock cart parade, the carriage parade, the water fête, the flower, fruit, and vegetable show, the fancy dress ball, the native *wayang* (theatres), the Malay fête, and the children's fête. The church bells were rung and a royal salute of twenty-one guns was fired from police headquarters (without disaster for the newly completed government office clock tower).

Those who entered for the fancy dress ball competition had to hand over a card 'on which should be clearly written their name and the character represented' and anyone who came to the ball not in fancy dress had to pay an entrance fee of $5.

The sporting events included a 'veterans' race' of 120 yards, for competitors aged 35 or more who had been at least '5 years in the East'. There was a competition for throwing a cricket ball the longest distance, a sack race, a tug-of-war (officials versus non-officials), a 'drop-kick' competition for Europeans and Eurasians (rugby football had just made its appearance), and a 1-mile bicycle race.

When the great day came, the main influx of sightseers into the town was through the railway station. 'Huge numbers . . . came in carriages, in cattle-trucks, in low-sides, in every imaginable vehicle which the Resident Engineer has devised to run upon rails . . . and so they went when all was over, having had four days without rain to spoil the out-door events.' Among many 'fringe'

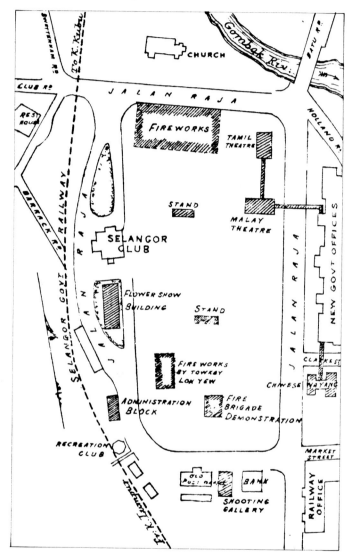

18. The Padang (Merdeka Square) showing the ground plan for
the Diamond Jubilee celebrations in June 1897, from the
Selangor Journal, 25 June 1897.

events Thambusamy Pillai gave a celebratory lunch at which 'curry and speeches were two of the principal features'. In the tug-of-war, the officials beat the unofficials ('comprising most of our well-known planters') by two bouts to one. At the Malay theatre, 'the principal feature was dancing to the strains of a fiddle . . . by little girls; the dresses worn by the various members of the troop were quaint and the stolid appearance of the small performers was extremely amusing . . . though the audience seemed to regard the matter as a rather serious one', anxious parents perhaps (SJ).

Making due allowance for the tact required of a reporter who has to live among those he reports on, everyone seems to have had fun.

6
More Serious Things

FOR Chinese of the pioneer generation, such as Yap Ah Loy, who had arrived in the 1860s, prospects of survival were very uncertain and, in their view, dependent on supernatural aid. Their religious tradition was eclectic. It could readily incorporate a patron deity of pioneers, Sze Ya (or Sen Ta), to whom Yap Ah Loy built a temple in 1864. The original shrine was replaced in 1882 by another, which still stood in modern times (though partly hidden by shophouses), near the junction of Jalan Tun H. S. Lee and Jalan Pudu. Sze Ya was a mythical figure related, rather like King Arthur or Robin Hood in English folk history, to a Chinese Mandarin, and, in Malaya, to a Capitan China of Sungei Ujong. These historical links, such as they are, are interesting examples of Chinese cultural ingenuity in adapting traditional stories to current needs.

A traditional Chinese deity 'is expected to render a return as the Roman gods were; a Roman observed his rites with scrupulous adherence to the letter of the law, expecting that if he did not the god would make it an excuse to wriggle out of the bargain, and', according to Purcell, 'the Chinese regard their gods in much the same spirit'.

Through the pages of the indispensable *Selangor Journal* we have a picture from another expert sinologue, Revd Fr. Charles Letessier, a Roman Catholic missionary in late nineteenth-century Kuala Lumpur, of the local religious observances of his time.

Sze Ya's reliability as an oracle had been established during the hard times of the civil war (1867–73) when his predictions provided the guide for strategic planning. In the years which followed the war, the sick, the gamblers, the traders, even the fallen women brought their problems to Sze Ya for advice. For a fixed and modest fee of fifty cents the priest consulted the God, going into a state of trance and 'articulating unintelligible sounds like the noise made by certain big jungle birds'. The acolytes interpreted 'this singular language', supplying a written prescription of the recommended remedy for the sick. It was reassuring, and for good measure, it was splendid entertainment.

In the same spirit the God was brought forth in annual procession, celebrated with extra pomp every seventh year. On these occasions the medium/priest was carried through the streets seated in 'a sedan chair which bristles with spikes'. The procession wended its way for several hours amid 'thousands of devout worshippers'.

The cult of Sze Ya was only one of several. Kuala Lumpur had a number of Chinese temples dedicated to different deities of the pantheon, as well as the assembly halls ('kongsi houses' to the Europeans) of various dialect groups—Hokkien, Hakka, Cantonese, etc.—who vied with each other in conspicuous expenditure (Colour Plate 10). In 1889, for example, a new temple had been built at a cost of $30,000.

The quieter and more austere religions of Muslim Malays and of Buddhist Sinhalese also had their places of worship, as has been mentioned in earlier chapters. The Jamek Mosque, which still stands at the confluence of the Gombak and Klang Rivers, on the site of what was originally a Muslim burial ground, was built in 1908–9. Sultan Sulaiman laid the foundation stone in 1908 in the presence of a large assembly of the principal Malays of the State and with full Muhammadan ritual. This was a period when Rulers of the various States vied with each other in building mosques. When the new mosque was completed, there was a second formal ceremony. In addition to a large concourse of Malays, the Resident and other officials attended the public ceremonial outside the building (Colour Plate 11).

In addition to the Sri Maha Mariamman Hindu temple, built by Thambusamy Pillai in central Kuala Lumpur, the Batu Caves, a few miles north of Kuala Lumpur, became a Hindu shrine known to all Hindus in Malaya and Singapore. Holland describes the festival celebrations: 'Thousands of Hindus, the healthy as well as the sick, the blind and the lame, and innumerable children, flock to celebrate the festival of Thaipusam. A fair is erected at the foot of the steps by the Sri Maha Mariamman Temple and many of the devotees bring offerings, including goats, to the Gods. The celebrations go on until late at night ... those who come to the caves are usually hot and tired when finally they reach the top of the steep steps. But at the Hindu Shrine one is able to obtain a cool and refreshing drink of pure cave water ... the sun's rays are most spectacular as they shine down through this hole [in the roof] illuminating the great cavern which is littered with huge boulders of limestone which in the past have fallen down from the roof.'

The first Christian (Anglican) Sunday services were held in the Residency from 1880 onwards, before there was a church building. The Resident, Bloomfield Douglas, had been a ship's master accustomed to taking services at sea. When Isabella Bird came to Klang in 1879 she attended a Residency service, such as Douglas continued after the move to Kuala Lumpur: 'The congregation sat under one punkah and the Resident under another ... everything was "shipshape" as becomes Mr Douglas's antecedents; a union jack over the desk, from which the liturgy was read, and a tiger skin over the tiles in front, the harmonium well played, and the singing and chanting excellent.'

However, Douglas could not prevail on his colleagues to plod up the hill to the Kuala Lumpur Residency, as there was a risk of being caught in a late afternoon rainstorm. He therefore moved the venue to the government offices, which were nearer to the staff bungalows, and attendance improved. A year or two later, the first church, a very modest building, was built near by in the Bluff Road area.

By 1890 the European and Eurasian population of Selangor had grown to about 200, though not all lived in Kuala Lumpur, and some were Roman Catholics who now had their own church at the Roman Catholic mission. But funds were raised to build a new Anglican church, the present St Mary's Cathedral. By now, many of the congregation came in pony traps and so the church was sited at the north end of the Padang (Merdeka Square) as the main centre of European communal activity. The design was first put out to open competition, but the results were unsatisfactory. The Government Architect, A. C. Norman, then prepared a Gothic design (see Colour Plate 16).

The move to build a new church owed something to the arrival, in 1890, of Revd Frank Haines, who combined the duties of chaplain and headmaster of the short-lived 'Raja School' for the education of young Malays of aristocratic family. Haines, who was a convivial man with a taste for amateur theatricals, later moved on to the chaplaincy at Penang, and was succeeded by a string of incumbents, none of whom stayed long. By now the chaplaincy had branched out into a 'Tamil mission', in the charge of a Tamil clergyman.

Attending the 11 a.m. Sunday service at St Mary's was a 'parade' and (wrote Edith Stratton Brown) 'all were expected to attend dressed as they would be in England—the men in tophats and long black coats, etc., the women of course in long silk or muslin dresses and hats or bonnets, gloves, etc. The Resident was always there and kept a sharp eye for any junior officer not present.' By now the Government Printer, John Russell, was a widower, but he brought his five young children to church on Sundays—among them the future founder of one of the most famous and long-lasting business houses of Selangor, J. A. Russell & Co.

By this time there were Roman Catholic, Methodist, and other churches and chapels, with congregations attending their own churches. In 1895 the Sanitary Board had to consider applications from a Mr Baird (denomination not given) to erect a 'mission hall' in Bluff Road and a 'Chinese gospel house' on Petaling Hill. Whereas the Anglican chaplain was an 'establishment' figure, to whose salary the State government made a contribution, the other clerics were essentially missionaries who proselytized among the non-Islamic communities, partly by doing excellent work in opening schools.

The French Roman Catholic priest, Charles Letessier, has already appeared as the chronicler of Chinese cults. Letessier had founded his mission and a primary school (on Bukit Nanas) in the early 1880s. He was also a pioneer in his work for the poor and distressed. He was particularly remembered as the founder (originally in the grounds of his mission) of a home for women— in fact, refugees from the brothels. Ill health forced him to leave Kuala Lumpur in 1899.

Although much of the secondary education provided in Kuala Lumpur at this time was centred on missions, the earliest and oldest surviving school, the Victoria Institution, was neither a denominational nor a government school. In 1887 funds had been raised to cover the costs of celebrating the Golden Jubilee of Queen Victoria, and when it was over there remained a sum of $3,188 unspent. It lay at the Treasury for some years so that it was to hand in 1893 when the Resident was William Treacher, who was later to take the lead in establishing the Malay College at Kuala Kangsar, in Perak, in 1905.

In Kuala Lumpur in 1893 the only secondary school was the Raja School, which had a dozen Malay pupils. Treacher lent a sympathetic ear to proposals from community leaders for founding a larger school, which would absorb the Raja School and admit pupils of all communities, comparable to the existing schools of the Straits Settlements towns. The Sultan, and several towkays, and the Selangor Government itself, made contributions to raise the jubilee fund to $21,641, of which $16,550 was spent in erecting the original buildings of the Victoria Institution, to be

19. St John's Institution (1906). (Steven Tan)

managed by a board of trustees. It became a government school and moved to a new site in the 1920s; in the 1890s the school stood at the southern end of the High Street, between that road and the Klang River. Revd Frank Haines was a likeable man but not a gifted teacher, so the post of headmaster of the Victoria Institution was filled by recruiting from England Bennett Shaw, who proved to be outstanding and fortunately remained with the school until 1922.

Although Fr. Letessier himself was forced by ill health to retire, he had founded a flourishing mission which, in 1904, established a boys' secondary school, the St John's Institution. Its initial enrolment of 42 pupils grew so rapidly that within two years, the Roman Catholic congregation, mainly Chinese, raised funds, augmented by a government grant, to erect an impressive school building for 500 pupils (Plate 19). This school, with the Victoria Institution and the Methodist Boys' School (p. 68), and later girls' schools too (p. 70) opened windows of opportunity for a new generation.

7
A New Era

As Kuala Lumpur moved into the twentieth century its destiny as a national capital was taking shape. It had become the capital of the Federated Malay States (Perak, Selangor, Negeri Sembilan, and Pahang) in 1896. But this had not been inevitable, despite the central position and commercial pre-eminence of Kuala Lumpur. Perak, as the premier State of the new federation, was rather miffed and the influential Sultan Idris of Perak, who became the senior Ruler on the death of Sultan Abdul Samad in 1898, and who had long been the spokesman of the Malay Rulers, continued to press the claims of his capital, Kuala Kangsar. He had insisted that the first gathering of FMS Rulers in 1897 should be held at Kuala Kangsar rather than at Kuala Lumpur. Again, when an FMS Federal Council (legislature) was established in 1909, its first meeting was held—with tremendous pomp—at Kuala Kangsar.

Kuala Lumpur did, however, stage the second assembly (durbar) of the four Rulers of the Federated Malay States in 1903—a much photographed occasion. The four Rulers and their retinue were accommodated in pavilions built in the Lake Gardens, each flying the distinctive flag of the State to which it was assigned. There was also a conference hall. The close of the meeting was celebrated by a procession of barges in the Lake Gardens. Sultan Idris of Perak, something of a showman, came downstream on the last float, resplendent in a military uniform—a little like the celebrated painting of Napoleon on the 'Bellerophon'.

An incidental consequence of Kuala Lumpur's status as a federal capital was the erection of yet more prestigious buildings (Colour Plate 12). In the Lake Gardens a large official residence was built for the senior federal administrator, the Resident-General. Its first occupant was Frank Swettenham, who by this time had some literary laurels; he had even joined Oscar Wilde, Aubrey Beardsley, and other lions of the naughty nineties in contributing to the notorious *Yellow Book*. It was Swettenham's fancy to call his new house 'Carcosa', a name taken from a poetic drama, *The King in Yellow*—'and beyond the towers of Carcosa rose behind the moon'. The reality was rather more prosaic—a mansion with seven bedrooms and nine bathrooms and spacious stables, which, after the end of colonial rule in 1957, was for some years used by the British High Commissioner (ambassador) as a gesture of appreciation by the independent government of Malaysia. It is now a hotel.

The Governor in Singapore doubled the role of High Commissioner in the Malay States and for him another large house was built, in 1913, alongside 'Carcosa'. This was called 'King's House' (since 'Government House' would have been inappropriate in a protected Malay State with its own Ruler). All the FMS Sultans, including Sultan Sulaiman of Selangor whose main *astana* (palace) was at Klang, had town houses in Kuala Lumpur. As the federal government grew, a sprawling collection of bungalows for bureaucrats was built on 'Federal Hill'. In this fashion, Kuala Lumpur emerged as the political capital of the Peninsula, though—as will be related—it was a painful process to bring all the Malay States into a single federation.

The FMS Hotel, the first in Kuala Lumpur, moved early in this century to what had been an annexe of the Selangor Club. Here it stood conveniently adjacent to the railway line and the trains stopped to pick up or deposit hotel guests (it was also close to the main European residential area) (Plate 20). Somewhat similar considerations impelled the railway management to include the Station Hotel, still standing, in the new central station building completed in 1911 (Colour Plate 13). Finally, in 1932, when the slump had made a new block of apartments opposite the station difficult to let, the building was adapted to become the Majestic Hotel. In the inter-war period, the FMS Hotel had ceased to be viable, but the Station Hotel and the Majestic faced each other as the leading first-class hotels of Kuala Lumpur, though many visitors stayed with friends (see, for example, Somerset Maugham at p. 62 below). A few lodging houses and boarding houses offered more modest attractions.

The main stimulus to the commercial growth of Kuala Lumpur

20. The FMS Hotel, formerly the Selangor Club annexe (see Plate 18), in 1906. (Antiques of the Orient)

was the rubber industry, which became the dominant influence soon after 1900. This followed the decline of the Selangor coffee plantations, which had begun in the 1880s and had a brief, hectic boom in the 1890s until killed off by disease and a drastic fall in the world price of coffee. When Ethel Hume arrived in Kuala Lumpur in 1899 by train from Klang, she looked out from 'the Resident's special carriage . . . to be rewarded by the sight of a regular tangle of jungle, interrupted every now and then by prim-looking coffee estates. [Her brother] explained that the coffee was Liberian, and, though very nice to drink, only fetched a miserable price in the market.' Coffee was also a demanding crop, which required partial shade from the tropical sun. Some planters had interplanted between their coffee bushes, to provide shade, a tree called *hevea brasiliensis*. This species had been enthusiastically promoted by the Director of the Singapore Botanic Gardens, H. N. Ridley ('Mad Ridley'), whose habit it was, when visited by coffee planters seeking advice, to slip seeds of the rubber tree into the pockets of their jackets, knowing that on return to their estates, these would be thrown out on the ground. That, at least, is a good story.

Certain it is that Ridley, later honoured as the father of the Malayan rubber industry, had to struggle against much opposition but the outcome proved that he was right.

There are competing claims for the credit of planting rubber as a commercial crop for the first time in Selangor. But one of the stronger claims is made for the Kindersley brothers, who are said to have planted 5 acres of rubber on their Inch Kenneth estate near Kajang, south of Kuala Lumpur, in 1895 or 1896. Those planters who, by design or good fortune, had planted rubber trees found them very profitable when in 1905, for the first but not the last time, the world price of rubber, driven by the new demand for motor-car tyres, rose to unimaginable levels. There was a mad rush to plant this wildly profitable crop, but the problem was found to be that, as it took about seven years to bring a rubber tree to the size at which it could be tapped for rubber, the world price had often fallen to disastrous levels by the time the new plantings came into bearing (Colour Plate 14). For a generation or more, the price of rubber fluctuated by up to 40 per cent in the course of some years.

The rubber planter, whether he had a pot of gold or a disaster on his hands, made his presence felt in Kuala Lumpur, although his estate was often at a distance from it. The French planter, Henri Fauconnier, wrote that at Kuala Lumpur 'the first Saturday of the month is Planters Day. They appear early in the morning, by every train and every road, to fetch the pay money [for the estate labourers] from the bank (Plate 21). The town awakes in agitation like a nest of white ants invaded by red ants. There is a new element in the air—gay, brutal, reckless. Voices are more resonant and rickshaws go faster. This access of fever lasts until midday.'

Then, hearing the execrated signal gun reverberate at midday, the planters moved in to their water-hole, the Selangor Club. Here, Fauconnier first had his hair trimmed 'by a magnificent Hindu, assisted by several apprentices ... aerial scissors clipped hypnotically round my head ... I felt as if all my troubles were dispelled'. Then, from the hairdressing salon to the crowded bar 'edged by an unbroken line of lifted elbows' he moved on to 'the

21. The labourers' roll-call on a rubber estate. (Steven Tan)

zone of occupation assigned to my district', i.e. the table at which the planters from Kuala Selangor gathered in uproarious conviviality.

It was not until after the First World War that motor cars came into general use, but a few enthusiasts had cars in Kuala Lumpur early in this century. It was Choo Kia Peng, earlier in his life when he worked for Loke Yew, who began his career as a motorist driving Loke Yew's cars. The first of these cars had to be started by lighting kerosene oil at the back to warm up the engine. It is hardly surprising that it caught fire in the centre of town: 'I jumped down, rushed to a Chinese shop and asked for an empty gunny rice-bag, and with it we extinguished the fire.' He then took 'the shortest way home' but it was only the beginning of some exciting adventures. Robson contributed to a handbook for visitors to Malaya a chapter of hints for motorists on tour: 'a revolver is not necessary, but there is no harm in carrying one'.

The majority of all communities preferred to play safe with a pony trap rather than expose themselves to the hazards of a 'motor velocipede'; the first of them to appear on the streets of Singapore was known informally as 'the coffee machine' (Colour

Plate 15). Planters sometimes used bicycles, which were coming into general use in the 1890s, to travel from their estates to the nearby metropolis of Kuala Lumpur.

There were other new, but quieter, professions in the town. Until 1896 the administrators had avoided incomprehensible technical arguments in the courts over which they presided by denying to professional advocates a 'right of audience'. They argued that poor litigants could not afford legal fees. Isabella Bird had sourly observed that 'a most queerly muddled system of law prevails under our flag ... but I have no doubt that justice is substantially done'.

Malay and Chinese dignitaries and officials continued to sit as magistrates or arbitrators in cases of which they had special knowledge of the local custom. But, with the expansion of commerce in Kuala Lumpur, there were cases in which substantial sums affecting investors in the Straits Settlements were at risk. In the early 1890s a maladroit decision on creditors' claims against an insolvent Selangor mining company left the Attorney-General of the Straits Settlements and the editor of *The Straits Times* (in their private capacity) the losers. The ensuing uproar was predictably rather noisier than usual. When the FMS was formed in 1896, a professional lawyer was appointed to fill a new senior judicial post, the 'Resident's courts' were abolished, and the ban on professional advocates was lifted. In October 1896 the *Selangor Journal* noted that 'Mr C. W. Hewgill, Advocate and Solicitor, has taken up residence in Kuala Lumpur. There are rumours of several other legal gentlemen coming here.'

Soon there were a number of local law firms, who congregated in Klyne Street (Jalan Lekiu), which became the Chancery Lane of Kuala Lumpur, just down the road from the law courts. It is a pity that Kuala Lumpur no longer commemorates John Klyne, the Eurasian surveyor who, in the 1880s, laid out much of the central area. The first Asian lawyer to practice in Kuala Lumpur was S. C. Goho, who set up in 1917. Meanwhile, the petition writer, pounding an ancient typewriter on the five-foot way, was still the poor man's lawyer.

We will leave the story of the doctors to the next chapter.

A growing population inevitably attracted and sheltered criminals. In 1895 the police had struggled for months to catch the Li Choi gang, 'their organisation being so perfect'. In their burglaries they went armed with 'revolvers of the latest pattern'. In the end Li Choi was caught, and eventually convicted of murder; he confessed that his spoils had included three government safes. In 1897 there were serious riots over government regulations made to prevent the use by street traders and shopkeepers of fraudulent balance scales (*dacing*). In 1909 the police fought an armed battle around the Pudu temple with a secret society gang which they had cornered. In 1912 came the most celebrated disturbance of all, the 'tauchang' (pigtail) riots. By this time the Malayan Chinese were reacting to the growing tide of reform in China; one of the most sensitive issues was the abandonment of the pigtail as a symbol of traditions which the reformers felt should be swept away. In some horseplay in Petaling Street at Chinese New Year, which got out of hand, a crowd dragged some rickshaw pullers into a barber's shop for the removal of what was—to their owners—a treasured appendage. The first fighting led on to paying off old scores between rival clans, so that the troops had to be called in to restore order.

As Kuala Lumpur moved on into the twentieth century, the pioneers who had lived in a small community on easy, though not intimate, terms with other communities were succeeded by a new generation of Europeans who were much more assertive of what they perceived as their superiority. In 1891 a total population of about 20,000 in Kuala Lumpur had included only some 150 Europeans, but by 1911 the figures were 47,000 and 1,396, a ten-fold expansion. With larger numbers and more European wives, the community became aloof. There were, of course, differences of behaviour; European women accompanied their husbands in the social round but Asian wives rarely did so (Plate 22). There were ugly episodes, such as a demand for segregation in first-class railway travel and hospital wards. It was all the sadder because the acknowledged leader of the Chinese at the time was Loke Yew, a man of great talent and charm who had travelled in Europe and who went so far as to produce a guide for his compatriots, advising them when travelling first-class, to avoid 'coarse talk', chewing

22. C. E. Spooner, General Manager of the Railway (*right*), his wife,
daughter, and son-in-law (D. G. Campbell) dressed up for his
investiture with the CMG, *c.*1907–10. (Airlie Gascoyne)

betel-nut, or taking off their shoes (see Plate 10). But in some
respects the efforts of the Westernized Asians to bridge the gap
were counter-productive; to wear the emperor's clothes was
resented.

The new cinema films from Hollywood, with their sometimes
erotic scenes, were felt to undermine the (overrated) status of the
European. In this tense situation the Ethel Proudlock case of 1911
was a bombshell. She was the wife of the acting headmaster of the
Victoria Institution who, on 23 April 1911, fired six shots from a
revolver into William Steward and killed him. At her trial her story
was that he had come uninvited to the house in her husband's
absence and had tried to rape her. She said that 'her hand came in

contact with' a revolver which was providentially on the table behind her. But after the first two shots he staggered out of the house and she followed and gave him four more as he lay on the ground. There was no trial by jury in the Malayan courts at this period (juries, especially if Asian, were felt to be unreliable) and so Mrs Proudlock was convicted by a court of a judge and two assessors, who plainly did not accept her story. It was conceded that she had met Steward the day before at the Club, though there was no evidence of their relationship. Amid a considerable uproar, the Sultan of Selangor granted her a pardon and she was bundled out of the country in haste.

In 1922 the celebrated writer Somerset Maugham visited Malaya, collecting material, and was the house guest of one of the lawyers who had defended Mrs Proudlock. The result was the most famous of all the author's Malayan short stories, 'The Letter', which varies the facts but undoubtedly is based on the Proudlock case. In his preface, Somerset Maugham disclaimed any intention to blacken the 'good, decent normal people' he met but few readers read prefaces. It is often worth looking behind the superb storytelling to the closely observed detail of the country and the lifestyle in these stories. At all events, Kuala Lumpur thus made an appearance in English literature—and it used to be said years afterwards that the bullet holes could be seen in the woodwork of the bungalow.

Far away in Europe events were moving to a climax which would do more than a local scandal to destroy the foundations of the old, secure scheme of things. When the news came of the outbreak of war, a delegation from the Selangor Chamber of Commerce called on the head of the FMS Government to propose a variety of emergency measures, such as mobilizing the FMS Volunteers, limiting withdrawals from the banks, controlling prices, and compulsory planting of food crops on rubber estates. Robson says that Sir Edward Brockman, an imperious bureaucrat, gave these ideas a 'polite but somewhat chilly reception'. It was to be business as usual.

However, it was no longer that kind of world. Suspension of trading on the London tin market precipitated a major crisis in

Kuala Lumpur, so that the government had willy nilly to buy all the local tin until normal markets were restored. The bombardment of Penang by the German cruiser *Emden*, in October 1914, was a nasty reminder that even the Royal Navy could not protect the sea lanes everywhere. There was worse to come. In February 1915 an Indian Army unit in Singapore, under orders to proceed elsewhere, mutinied, released some rather bewildered German prisoners, and turned on its officers and local civilians, killing forty-four. It was soon over but the Raj seemed shaky; further afield than Kuala Lumpur, the Sultan of Kelantan did not conceal from his British Adviser his doubts as to the outcome of the war. However, in time Malaya settled down to a long, long haul to November 1918, with the editor of the *Malay Mail* interpreting the cables to make it 'the most optimistic journal in Malaya'.

8
Between the Wars

THE brave new post-war world began disastrously. There was an abrupt cessation of industrial use of rubber for military vehicles and the new areas planted with rubber during the hectic boom of 1910 came into bearing. There was massive unemployment on estates and mines, which the government proposed to relieve by repatriation to China and India. Choo Kia Peng remembered how 'people used to rush into the office [of the Secretary for Chinese Affairs] in High Street . . . some of them tried to rush through the windows. In the first two or three months we must have repatriated 30,000 Chinese labourers alone.' All employers, public and private retrenched drastically. Although the 1932 slump lasted longer, that of 1921 was regarded as the worst. It was the beginning of recurrent cycles of boom and bust which lasted for most of the years between the wars.

There was endless, but fruitless, discussion at meetings of the FMS Federal Council in Kuala Lumpur of proposals to make the FMS constitution loose enough to accommodate the other five Unfederated Malay States (UMS) as additional members. In the end, this had to await the post-war reconstruction of 1946–8. While the bureaucratic Punch and Judy show on 'decentralization' went on, local opinion hoped that Kuala Lumpur, as the capital of the federation, would escape from the shadow of the political and commercial domination of Singapore. This was a sign of changing attitudes, and so it was gratifying that, for the first time, a British 'royal' (the future King Edward VIII) included Kuala Lumpur in his Malayan itinerary in 1922, even if 'some of the good ladies of Kuala Lumpur were a little anxious about their proficiency in the curtsying business'.

Another sign of the rising status of Kuala Lumpur came in 1925 when Rotary International, hearing that there were plans for founding 'a non-communal social club, where men and women of various races could meet on an equal footing', sent an envoy to state the case for making it a Rotary Club. By now the sour atmosphere of the Edwardian period had passed; the Kuala Lumpur Rotary Club was launched with a dinner at the 'Chinese millionaires club' with the Resident as the first president. It was a great success.

Arthur Keyser, returning after an absence of twenty years, noted that Malays 'alas! ride in motor cars, wearing patent leather shoes and spats'. This was unfair on the Malays, few of whom owned motor cars (or spats) in comparison with the generally more affluent motorists of other communities. But for those who had them, dashing about in cars, especially to social occasions, was now the accepted tempo and style of living.

The most dramatic event of the period was the flood of December 1926 (Plate 23). There had been floods before. In 1913, for example, a Kuala Lumpur lawyer won a bet by swimming from the steps of the long bar veranda of the Selangor Club to the King Edward VII statue under the clock tower (of the Bangunan Sultan Abdul Samad) without putting foot to ground. But December 1926 was 'the mother and father' of all floods. As the water rose, the staff of the Chartered Bank made frantic, but unavailing, efforts to keep the water out of the vaults. When the flood subsided, notes to the value of several million dollars were taken from the treasury to be dried in the open air under the eyes of the armed guard. After that, a much more drastic straightening of the river channel created an effective outlet for the flood water coming down from the hills above Kuala Lumpur. It was tested successfully by the floods of 1930 when a tiger was observed in mid-stream being swept downriver at speed—the last occasion when a tiger at liberty—more or less—was seen in central Kuala Lumpur.

Kuala Lumpur had begun with a tragedy—the death from malaria of eighty-seven Chinese pioneers. It was a debt repaid in this century. In 1901 the young medical officer at Klang, Dr (later Sir Malcolm) Watson, found that by exposing the drainage channels to sunlight, the breeding of mosquitoes and the local incidence of malaria was dramatically reduced. However, when Watson's methods were applied to newly cleared building areas

23. The Java Street (Jalan Tun Perak) bridge under water in the 1926 flood, from Sidney, *c*.1926.

(Federal Hill) in Kuala Lumpur, the number of mosquitoes actually increased.

There were some zany theories duly recorded in the history of the Institute of Medical Research. One expert advocated stunning mosquito larvae, like fish, with underwater explosions. In a laboratory experiment, Chinese crackers were lit under a tin of water full of larvae. We learn that 'the water was spilt but the larvae were unharmed'. Eventually, it was found that the mosquitoes prevalent in inland districts are a different species from those of the coast and multiply in different breeding conditions. To deal with the concentrated Kuala Lumpur problem, 248 miles of subsoil drains were installed over 32 square miles (the man who carried it through was known as 'Drainpipe Evans' thereafter) and within ten years the death rate from malaria halved (Plate 24). But this technique is uneconomic except in towns. However, Watson came back from the Panama Canal zone where he had pioneered a new technique and found, to his surprise, that it worked in rural areas of Malaya. It was the spraying of a thin film of oil on open drains so that the larvae cannot come up to breathe. Thus, Kuala Lumpur (and its Institute of Medical Research) has its place in the world-wide campaign against malaria.

From the same source comes the story of another doctor, Ernest Travers, remembered for his work among the lepers. The lepers of

24. Laying drains to check the breeding of malaria-carrying mosquitoes, from Hodder, 1959. (Crown copyright photograph)

Kuala Lumpur were for many years confined to an 'asylum' adjoining the Pauper Hospital—'a thieves kitchen, which had the reputation for the best forgeries of notes and coin and the most potent illicit liquor in the country, the skilled leper forgers and distillers being completely undisturbed. Few of the inhabitants of the houses surrounding the leper asylum could keep a bath tub, for more than a few weeks, these being stolen by the lepers for preparing the "mash" from which the local samsu (spirit) was distilled.'

When Travers took charge 'some 400 men, women and children were confined under the most wretched conditions. Neither clothes, nor blankets were provided for them . . . they were constantly escaping into the town in spite of all possible precautions, and they stole anything they could lay their hands on from the neighbouring houses. In the asylum itself disturbances and riots were a weekly occurrence, and no official dared even enter into it without a guard. Travers changed all this in an incredibly short time . . . instead of having to prevent the lepers from escaping, the difficulty was to house those who came from all parts of the country for the new treatment.' The eventual permanent solution, which owed much to Travers' advocacy, was an agricultural settlement for lepers at Sungei Buloh, a few miles north of Kuala Lumpur, where they could live more or less normal lives while under treatment (Plate 25).

After the Victoria Institution had been founded in 1893, the secondary schools were mainly the work of the missionaries, such as the American Methodist, W. E. Horley, who arrived in 1904 to take charge of the Methodist Boys' School. When he took over, the school was accommodated in an old fruit market building in Malacca Street in the Malay quarter. It then moved to a mission hall in Sultan Street, but by 1905 it could move into a new school designed for 400 boys. In addition to being a first-class school for English-medium teaching, it was unusual in including in its curriculum daily lessons in vernacular languages. Horley was still at his school in the 1920s—a bluff personality, who overcame all obstacles, even lack of money—he regularly preached in Chinese.

That aspect of Horley explains why men (and also women

25. Leper patients taking their medicine, *c.*1925, from Sidney, 1926.

missionaries) of Horley's type achieved so much. In the tradition of mission work in China, they set out to identify themselves with the community among whom they worked, so that their churches and schools won the support, including gifts of money, of the people who came to church and sent their children to school.

However, by 1920 the schools, starved of money and staff during the war, were in need of new methods and ideas. In that year the Education Department noted that many candidates taking the leaving examination 'seemed to look on "apprenticeship" as a kind of boat'. Shakespeare was studied 'with elaborate care and attention to archaic expressions'. The mould was broken by a new generation of teachers. The Victoria Institution gave performances of Shakespeare plays, which demonstrated both to pupils and to the public that they were realistic and even funny (Plate 26). Classes were taken to rubber estates and tin mines to replace the abstruse study of Canadian wheat yields.

26. Shakespeare's *Twelfth Night*—the final scene—at the Victoria Institution, *c.*1925, from Sidney, *c.*1926.

One of the most innovative teachers was Josephine Foss, head-mistress of a girls' school at Pudu on the outskirts of Kuala Lumpur. Faced with the official view that a little arithmetic might 'feed the minds' of her girls but their real vocation was 'marriage and motherhood', she insisted upon wider horizons. Her school became a centre of excellence, teaching the natural sciences and commercial subjects to the senior classes. Her battle cry was 'educate the Asian girls and they'll be just as good, if not better than the Western girls'. Like 'Mad Ridley', with his rubber seeds, she lived to be vindicated by the result. Revisiting Pudu in 1963 at the age of seventy-six, she had a rapturous welcome from some 600 of her former pupils, many of them professional women, including some of the first to qualify in medicine.

This is much more than the story of a handful of talented and dedicated Europeans with their individual achievements. Pupils need jobs; technical services need trained staff. In 1906 a Technical College was established in Kuala Lumpur to train staff for public works, surveying, railways, etc. It was ahead of its time and indeed closed for ten years from 1914 because, it was said, it did not attract pupils in sufficient numbers. At Serdang, not far from Kuala Lumpur, there was a College of Agriculture, with rubber and forestry research institutes elsewhere around the town, whose functions included training. Teacher training at this period was mainly based on apprenticeship ('normal class') methods. The only medical college was in Singapore, which—in Raffles College—had the embryo university. In retrospect, it may seem inadequate and poorly designed. But it was a beginning and it began to produce a new generation of Malayans equipped for a new and dynamic post-war development.

The year 1937 saw the prices of rubber and tin rise again to their highest levels for almost a decade, but relative prosperity did not bring peace of mind. A strike by the coalminers at Batu Arang, near Kuala Lumpur, was quickly ended but it moved the police to an apocalyptic warning in an official report that 'the Federated Malay States had passed through the most serious crisis in its history. It was within an ace of dissolving into temporary chaos as a result of communist intrigue. Had the organisation not been crushed this country . . . would have been in very serious danger of being overrun by angry and desperate Chinese mobs.' There was further trouble in 1941 among Indian labourers on estates to the west of the town. The long, hard years of slump and massive unemployment, unrelieved (as it had been in 1921) by large-scale repatriation, had made the working-class very restless. Official fears of communist infiltration induced a policy of legal prohibition of trade unions. Much else contributed to the uprising in 1948 known as the Emergency, but there is a case for tracing its origins to the decade before the war.

Political activity was unfocused. The Malayan Chinese were much troubled by events in China and formed an Anti-Enemy Backing Up Society (AEBUS) to boycott Japanese goods. Josephine Foss was asked by her Chinese friends not to use the hairdresser at the Selangor Club because, although the best in town, he was Japanese. The Indian community, riven as so often by internal feuds, was preoccupied with the Congress campaign in India for self-government.

For the Malays, there was no external distraction. The small but influential urban middle-class of civil servants and a handful of lawyers and journalists was drawn into a Malaya-wide movement to protect and assert Malay rights, threatened by immigrant communities. On a Sunday morning in June 1938, some 400 Malays gathered at the Sultan Sulaiman Club in Kampung Bahru to form a Selangor Malay Association. It was all very subdued and restrained. Among those present was Raja Uda, a member of the Selangor ruling dynasty and a senior Malay civil servant. After the war he was to become the Chief Minister of Selangor as the representative of the United Malays National Organization (UMNO). In 1938 that lay a long way ahead but they had crossed the Rubicon.

When the war came in September 1939 the unease grew. British and Commonwealth troops appeared in Kuala Lumpur, and it was reassuring to think of the new naval base in Singapore. Digging air raid shelters proved difficult in the low-lying areas of swampy ground in Kuala Lumpur. The Japanese hairdresser, and many of his compatriots in the town—photographers and the like—arranged to take indefinite leave in Japan. The local St John's Ambulance organized medical training courses for volunteers and 'many young Asian men went to A.R.P. classes'. When the invasion began in December 1941 the wounded came down by train from the north and schoolgirls, of sixteen and above, volunteered as nurses in the wards of the General Hospital. Japanese aircraft dropped leaflets—'Join the Japs, Asia for the Asians.'

Japanese troops entered Kuala Lumpur on 12 January 1942 with heavy clouds of 'inky smoke' rising over the town from burning stocks of rubber. A new era and a grim ordeal for Kuala Lumpur had begun.

Retrospect from the 1990s

THE author of this brief history lived in Kuala Lumpur for eight years (1948–56) but, on his latest return in 1991, thought it wise to buy a street guide in case he should get lost in an unfamiliar town. The change in the physical layout and appearance of Kuala Lumpur, especially over the past twenty years, is striking and—to the returning resident—bewildering.

Like other cities of the world, Kuala Lumpur has responded to increased demand for land by building up to the sky. As architecture, the resulting skyscrapers are of varying quality, but collectively the business heart of Kuala Lumpur differs little in its jagged skyline from, say, downtown Los Angeles (Colour Plate 16). The insistent pressure of the motor car, in vast numbers, chokes the city and multilane highways are a response to the pressure and not a solution. In the course of building these structures, much of the old town has been demolished and what remains is often dwarfed by the sheer scale of the new city.

Yet, there is no going back. As the Roman poet Horace noted, 'Times change and we change with them.' This is the Kuala Lumpur of the modern age. If its citizens groan a little at some of its features, this is their lifestyle. The city could not be the capital of a prosperous and progressive nation state in any other way.

All that the historian can suggest—and this is the theme of these pages—is that the modern age should understand that it has been the heir to a community which left its legacy. Even now, it is there to be seen in places, and where it can be preserved, it should be cherished. This is not mere nostalgia. There are authorities such as the Bandaraya (Municipality) and bodies such as the Badan Warisan Malaysia (Heritage of Malaysia Trust) which have done good work to conserve and explain the relics of the past to the citizen and the visitor of these days. May it continue so.

Select Bibliography

Bird, Isabella L., *The Golden Chersonese and the Way Thither*, John Murray, London, 1883; reprinted Oxford University Press, Kuala Lumpur, 1967 and 1980.

Brown, Edith Stratton, 'Looking Back on Selangor in the Nineties', in *Fifty Years of Progress 1904–1954*, Malay Mail Supplement, 1955.

Butcher, John G., *The British in Malaya 1880–1941: The Social History of a European Community in South-East Asia*, Oxford University Press, Kuala Lumpur, 1979.

Choo Kia Peng, 'My Life's Journey', unpublished autobiography, c.1953.

Coote, Philip C., *Peeps at Many Lands: The Malay States*, A. & C. Black, London, 1923.

Fauconnier, Henri, *The Soul of Malaya* (trans. by Eric Sutton), George Allen & Unwin, London, 1931; reprinted Oxford University Press, Kuala Lumpur, 1985.

Gullick, John M., 'Kuala Lumpur 1880–1895', *Journal of the Malayan Branch of the Royal Asiatic Society*, Vol. 28, Pt. 4, 1955.

———, *The Story of Kuala Lumpur (1857–1939)*, Eastern Universities Press, Singapore, 1983.

———, *Josephine Foss and the Pudu English School: A Pursuit of Excellence*, Pudu English School Old Girls' Association, Kuala Lumpur, 1988.

———, 'The Growth of Kuala Lumpur and of the Malay Community in Selangor before 1880', *Journal of the Malaysian Branch of the Royal Asiatic Society*, Vol. 63, Pt. 1, 1990.

Harrison, Cuthbert Woodville, *An Illustrated Guide to the Federated Malay States*, 4th edn., Malay States Information Agency, London, 1923.

Hodder, B. W., *Man in Malaya*, University of London Press, London, 1959.

Holland, E. G., *A Guide to Batu Caves*, Donald Moore, Singapore, 1955.

Hornaday, William T., *Two Years in the Jungle: The Experiences of a Hunter and Naturalist in India, Ceylon, the Malay Peninsula and Borneo*, Charles Scribner's Sons, New York, 1885; reprinted as *The Experiences of a Hunter and Naturalist in the Malay Peninsula and Borneo*, Oxford University Press, Kuala Lumpur, 1993.

Hume, Ethel Douglas, *The Globular Jottings of Griselda*, William Blackwood & Sons, Edinburgh, 1907.

Institute for Medical Research, *Fifty Years of Medical Research in Malaya 1900–1950*, Government Press, Kuala Lumpur, 1951.

Keyser, Arthur L., *People and Places: A Life in Five Continents*, John Murray, London, 1922.

Letessier, Revd Fr. Charles, 'Si Sen Ta—A Chinese Apotheosis', *Selangor Journal*, Vol. 1, 1893.

Lim, Jon H. S., 'Shophouse Rafflesia', *Journal of the Malaysian Branch of the Royal Asiatic Society*, Vol. 66, Pt. 1, 1993.

Middlebrook, Stanley M., 'Yap Ah Loy', *Malayan Branch of the Royal Asiatic Society*, Vol. 24, Pt. 2, 1951.

Ng Seo Buck, 'Some Recollections of Kuala Lumpur Fifty Years Ago', *Malayan Historical Journal*, Vol. 1, Pt. 1, 1954.

Pasqual, J. C., 'Chinese Tin Mining', *Selangor Journal*, Vol. 4, 1896.

Pertubuhan Akitek Malaysia, *Guide to Kuala Lumpur: Notable Buildings*, Kuala Lumpur, 1986.

Purcell, Victor W., *The Chinese in Malaya*, Oxford University Press, London, 1948.

Rathborne, Ambrose B., *Camping and Tramping in Malaya: Fifteen Years Pioneering in the Native States of the Malay Peninsula*, Swan Sonnenschein, London, 1898; reprinted Oxford University Press, Singapore, 1984.

Robson, John H. M., *Records and Recollections 1889–1934*, Kyle Palmer, Kuala Lumpur, 1934.

Scrivenor, J. B., *A Sketch of Malayan Mining*, Mining Publications Ltd., London, 1928.

Selangor Golf Club, *Twelve under Fours: An Informal History of the Selangor Golf Club*, 1953.

Sidney, Richard J. H., *In British Malaya To-day*, Hutchinson, London, c.1926.

———, *Malay Land Tanah Malayu*, Palmer, London, 1926.

Swettenham, Sir Frank A., *British Malaya: An Account of the Origin and Progress of British Influence in Malaya*, John Lane, London, 1907; rev. edn. Allen & Unwin, London, 1948.

———, *Footprints in Malaya*, Hutchinson, London, 1942.

Swettenham, Sir Frank A., Burns, P. L., and Cowan, C. D. (eds.), *Sir Frank Swettenham's Malayan Journals*, Oxford University Press, Kuala Lumpur, 1975.

Wright, A. and Cartwright, H. A., *Twentieth Century Impressions of British Malaya*, Lloyds Publishing, London, 1908.

Contemporary writing in the *Selangor Journal*, the *Straits Times* and the *Singapore Free Press*, official records, and personal memoirs have also provided material.

Index

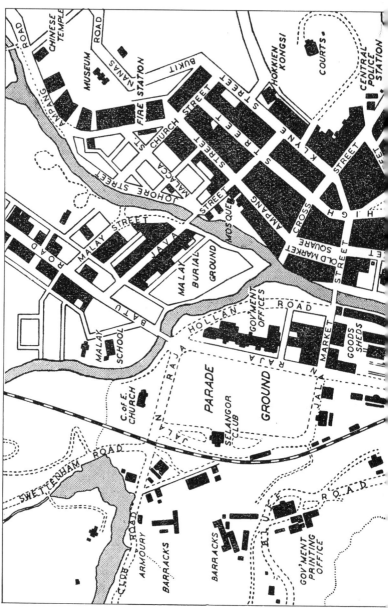

Kuala Lumpur in 1895. Redrawn by K. M. Foong from a map prepared by the Federal Town Planning Department (1950). (Reproduced by permission of the Malaysian Branch of the Royal Asiatic Society)